I'm Somebody Important

GEORGE MITCHELL

I'M SOMEBODY IMPORTANT

Young Black Voices from Rural Georgia

UNIVERSITY OF ILLINOIS PRESS   Urbana Chicago London

To Alison Ceplikas

Preface

The victims of oppressive social forces in this nation are rarely known in human terms by their more fortunate fellow citizens. Few of those who reap the benefits of this affluent society think of them in the same way that they might think of their own relatives, neighbors, or business associates. One reason is that the mass of printed and filmed material about them available to everyone does not often enough depict them as individual human beings with whom one could really identify or for whom one could feel any emotion — except, sometimes, pity. Government reports picture them in terms of cold statistics; scholarly studies usually portray them in abstract analyses as members of a group with certain "characteristics"; feature stories in the mass media often show them only as poor folks deserving pity for their plight.

The purpose of this book, then, is to allow the reader to get to know in human terms some of the victims of America's great social ills of racism and poverty — in this case six young black people who live in the rural South. In their own words they describe their aspirations, frustrations, loves, hates, opinions, and uncertainties, and these thoughts and feelings are not always influenced by their status as victims of racism and poverty — though they often are — and they are not always unlike those of anyone else — though they sometimes are.

Poor black people in *rural* areas were asked to talk about themselves because in recent years they not only have been ignored as real individuals with human motivations and feelings but have been ignored altogether. Concern over the problems of racism and poverty is focused almost exclusively on urban ghettos, which leads one to conclude that the conscience of the affluent sector of this society is aroused only when it is threatened. Harmful drugs were not defined as an urgent problem until the children of the well-to-do began using them, although they had been a part of the scene for years among many of the poor. Likewise, poverty and racism are considered urgent problems only in the big cities, which just may be leveled if these forms of oppression are not eradicated. But black people in rural areas, who suffer from the same oppression, offer no threat, and so they and their problems are ignored.

In recent years many black people — with reason — have become upset about the large number of white scholars and authors who have gone into their communities to do studies and write books about them. They point out that most of these studies and books are racist in nature and have not resulted in action to help the people they are about. As Gene Marine wrote from the white standpoint in *Playboy,* "How can I look at you as a problem, and propose measures to solve that problem, unless somehow I regard myself as the better or wiser of us?"

The justifications I can offer for yet another book about black people by a white person hinge on the fact that I did not look upon the people I was interviewing as problems needing analysis. I thought of them just as people — people who I thought should have the opportunity to present themselves. The book, therefore, is in their own words.

I did produce the book, however, with the presumption that there *is* a problem. But the people who speak on these pages are not the problem; their predicament is its end result. To me, the "poverty cycle" is not the problem; the "breakdown of the family structure" is not the problem. These are only symptoms of the real problem, which is a system that encourages racism, greed, materialism, exploitation, and refusal to look upon one's fellow human beings as brothers.

So one of my reasons for writing this book was that I hoped it might urge a few readers to take meaningful and, hopefully, radical action to reform the system and to help its victims. And I don't believe that most government reports, scholarly analyses, or sob stories in newspapers alone can do this — not only because they all too often do not recognize the real problem but also because the people they are about are not introduced to readers as human beings with whom they can identify. It seems to me that few persons can become concerned enough for oppressed people to attempt to upset the status quo and possibly their own lives to help them, unless they feel they know some of them in a personal way. Whether this book can lead toward such a goal, I do not know.

Neither do I know everything that should be done to reform the system and to help its victims. But I *do* know that present programs and laws are not sufficient. It is not only that they do not attack root causes; they do not even do what they were designed to. Civil rights laws on employment, housing, and public accommodations are hardly ever heeded in the areas where the young people in this book live. The local agencies of the Office of Economic Opportunity touch only one of their lives. Even organizations in the black movement have not moved into these young people's areas, much less recruited them for the battle (which would be an ideal constructive outlet for their youthful energies). To successfully solve the problems, insuring that these programs and laws do what they were designed to do would be a small step in the right direction. A reordering of national priorities and a national commitment to eradicating poverty and racism are a must. And revolutionary changes in cultural values and in the social, political, and economic system will probably be necessary.

But there is one prerequisite for any action taken. James M. Wall put it well in *South Today:* "The acceptance — assumed acceptance, not just reasoned acceptance — of blacks as human beings . . . is essential to the overcoming of a national racism that functions primarily because whites have managed to deny the humanity of invisible blacks in their midst."

Finally, why did I choose *young* black people to tell their stories? They were born in a period when racial discrimination and oppression were generally accepted, and they grew up in a period when a full-scale movement against discrimination and oppression raged. And they are coming into adulthood in a period that is beginning with a grave question: Will they and the thousands like them be able to build lives for themselves and their children in a society that recognizes them as equal human beings?

The first task in producing this book was to locate the authors. The only qualifications I had in mind were that they had to be young and black, to live in rural areas and be members of families whose economic status was typical for rural blacks, and to be willing to be interviewed about every major facet of their lives. There was one other crucial necessity. The youths would have to consider me — a white man — a partner in this venture instead of a "bossman." Had their growing-up experiences in the most oppressive of racist atmospheres made meaningful communication between them and a white man impossible? Some of my urban friends and associates — both white and black — predicted that this would indeed be the case. But I hoped that if I considered them my partners, they would consider me theirs, and so the barriers that have been built so high over the past few hundred years could be broken down far enough to yield a book that would enable the reader to really get to know the young people.

Finding young black people from poor rural families who were willing to participate in the project proved to be no problem. In fact, everyone I told about the idea was anxious to be a part of it. All of the six who can be seen and heard in this book were introduced to me by adults the young people knew and respected.

The six young people, all but one of whom were in their teens, live near or in four small towns with average populations of about 2,000 in an area of southwest Georgia known as the lower Chattahoochee Valley, one of the most poverty-stricken regions in the country. All live far enough away (from thirty-five to eighty-five miles) from the valley's major city, Columbus, to say accurately that they live in rural areas. Few industries have located in the rural counties of the valley, and farming now provides a livelihood for relatively few families. The major economic activities in the region center around pulpwood and peanuts, and many of the poor earn their meager livings from these products.

My fears that the young people might be unable or unwilling to communicate with me — to talk about themselves, to reveal their feelings and attitudes, to "open up" — proved to be largely unfounded. I did find it necessary to drop from the project two of the eight with whom I began interviews. These two were from the poorest families (the father of one supported a family of thirteen on the thirty-five dollars a week he made at the rate of fifty cents an hour) and were the most retarded in school (one was fifteen years old and in the sixth grade, the other sixteen and in the seventh grade). Both experienced great difficulty responding to simple questions, and I believe this was due to both racial barriers and lack of verbal ability.

But the six young persons whose stories and pictures compose this book seemed on the whole to express themselves freely. I believe they did so because of several factors. To be asked to tell about themselves for a book made them aware of their importance as individuals and citizens of this country; they were glad to have the opportunity to present their views to others; and they considered me, at least in some ways, as a friend.

In introducing the project, I told them they would be writing their own book and they could decline to answer any question they wished or could answer it with the understanding that it would not appear in the book. I also explained that the book's purpose was to enable the reader to get to know them in human terms, which might in some small way contribute to an improvement in the racial and economic situations of poor black people. And after they agreed to be interviewed, I told them they would share in the book's profits by receiving two dollars an hour for talking to me and by equally dividing 60 percent of the royalties if there were any after my total expenses had been met.

All six seemed to enjoy the interviews, and at least a couple were genuinely disappointed when we had finished. For all except one, who had to leave town shortly after I met him, the interviews were conducted twice weekly over a one-month period during the spring and summer of 1970, in a relaxed, informal atmosphere at their homes. Although I had a list of questions I asked everyone, most of my questions sprang from answers to previous questions. I volunteered to answer any questions about myself they might want to ask, but their questions were usually confined to my wife and what she was like. My questions, to say the least, were not confined. They were asked to talk about everything from their girl-friends and boyfriends to their solutions to today's racial problems.

In regard to what social scientists call "interviewer bias," I tried not to ask leading questions, to put words into their mouths, or to express my own opinions on issues I was asking about. But it should be remembered that simply my presence would have to color some of their comments. That I am white instead of black, that I am middle-class instead of lower-class, that I am young instead of old, that I am male instead of female, that I have a moustache instead of being clean-shaven — all of these factors and more undoubtedly influenced them. And many of the questions I put to them had never before consciously crossed their minds.

The book's presentation of the interviews also requires explanation. When the job of editing sat before me after more than four months of interviewing and transcribing tapes, I reached the decision neither to present the interviews in their original, somewhat chaotic, form nor to neatly organize them by subject matter. The former would lack coherence, which any writer must give to his work to some degree. Too much coherence, too much organization of the young peoples' thoughts and feelings, however, would not give a true picture of them, or any other human being for that matter. A human's mind does not work like a machine; it does not separate its work into neat little compartments; it has no problem producing contradictions.

So I decided to compromise. I edited the interviews by arranging them in loose categories of subject matter. Yet through various methods I tried to retain the original mood, and to keep every statement in its original context, as well as I could. (At this point, it might be useful to point out that any contradictory statements appearing within a chapter are in the order in which they were made.)

I consider the photographs an integral part of this work because I believe they are necessary for the reader to become as intimately acquainted with these young people as possible without actually meeting them. The photographs in each chapter were taken at the home or "hangout" of the person in that chapter, and most of the people in the photographs are members of his or her family.

The names of people and places other than well-known persons and large cities have been changed.

I owe thanks to many people: first and most important, the six who actually wrote the book; Mrs. Navy Lou Epps, Mrs. Nanny Jenkins, and Mrs. Mamie Kendrick for introducing me to them; Rene Beiring for helping with the transcribing and typing; Randy Chapell for processing film; Wes Jones for photographic advice; Dr. Robert Coles for his encouragement; and my wife, Cathy, for printing the photographs and for doing a lot more, including originating the idea for the book and keeping up my spirits as I struggled to translate that idea into reality.

Contents

Betty Brown   3

Felton Jones   45

Janice Riley   89

Sammy Jackson   127

Rosie Mae Davis   167

Bobby Gaines   197

I'm Somebody Important

Betty Brown

Betty Brown lives with her mother, stepfather, brother, and sister in a two-room shack next to the railroad tracks in Adamsville, Georgia. Less than half a mile away reside the wealthy of the town in huge white mansions and split-level brick homes. Betty is fourteen years old but looks and comports herself as if she were seventeen or eighteen. She talks vivaciously; her eyes twinkle saucily when her mood is light and blaze when she is angry.

My grandmother, she raised me. You know, I was staying with her from the time I was born, all while I was small until she died, and then I started staying with my mother. See, my mother and my real father, they wasn't married, and my mother didn't marry until about two or three years after I was born. When she was first married, she stayed at my grandmother's for a while, and then they got their own house.

— Did you want to live with your mother or grandmother?

My grandmother. I don't know why I didn't want to live with my mother. I went to spend the night with her sometime. I don't think I liked my stepfather. They used to fight a lot and on like that. You know, I spend the night with them sometime on the weekend, and they get to fighting. I be crying, but it didn't do no good.

But my grandmother was real nice, she was friendly to everybody, she didn't never get mad at nobody, but she was stingy, you know, she kept money, she wouldn't hardly spend no money. She worried a lot about her children, she was a Christian, she went to church all the time.

I was about five or six years old when she died. The way she died, she was getting up out of bed, and you know the pot, the slop jar, you know what you urinate in — she always kept it 'side of the bed so she wouldn't have to go outside . . . Well, anyway, she got up fixing to get ready to go to work and she went to sit on that, but she missed it and fell on the floor. And then I started crying and woke Mr. Jimmy up — that was her husband — and he said he thought she was dead. He told me to go find my mama and my aunt and tell them. So I got them. She was dead. Doctor said she had a heart attack. I though she just missed the pot and fell on the floor.

•   •   •

I wish my mother had never married my stepfather, 'cause I don't like him that much. I don't like how he get drunk and go on and he don't seem to have too much responsibility when he drunk and I don't like that, and I wish she hadn't married him.

Bo Dad, that's what everybody calls him and I do too, he always get drunk. If anybody'll let him have some money to buy some. Peoples sell liquor in their house, corn liquor. He drinks that stuff all the time. Through the week when he be working, he don't get drunk too much. He mostly get drunk on the weekends and when it be raining, he don't go to work, he gets drunk. He be all right when he comes home from work. He be tired, you know.

But them other days he'll worry you to death. If anybody come up here, he be bugging 'em for money. He be messing with me, and I'll knock him down, keep a'going! I can knock him down. I have knocked him down, or either he was drunk and just fell, one. Yeah, if he make me mad, I hit him. Knock him out. We'll get to fighting. He hits me and I'll hit him with my fist and anything else. With a broom, shoes, glass, bottle, anything. Like if he come in drunk, you know, and jump on my mama, then I jump in. I be trying to separate 'em, you know. And then he'll get mad, and me and him will start. And sometimes we fight if he just be bothering me. He be messing with me, you know, pulling me and hitting me for no reason at all.

And he know I hate that they married. And I've told him. I say I wish Betty — that's my mama — I say I wish she hadn't married him, and I can't stand him. I like him when he's sober — he's real quiet then, don't have much to say — I like him then. But when he get drunk, good God!

— Do you wish your mother were married to your real father?

No! Because I wouldn't be able to go nowhere. You know, not go like I go now. Because he's sort of tight. When I visited him in Atlanta, he wouldn't let me do much of nothing. Crazy 'bout him, but no!

— How do you feel about them not ever getting married?

I think that he should of married her when she got pregnant with me. She wanted him to then, but after denying it and saying I wasn't none of his child, she didn't want to. Then after I was born he wanted to marry her — that's what she said. But before I was born, he didn't, so she wouldn't marry him.

•   •   •

I get along better with my mother than my stepfather. We don't hardly ever get to fussing. And I can talk to her with my problems or come to her with my problems and talk to her and ask her advice and she'll give it to me. Mostly I ask her about boys. I ask do she think that I should go with a boy that got a baby by another girl. Why is it wrong for a young girl to go with a married man. Things like that.

But I don't get along with my stepfather too good. We argue about anything. Like if he's fussing or hitting at my mama, then I'll jump in and we get to arguing. See, he jealous of her. He accuse her of going with this man in this neighborhood. Like this man be going down this road and she be standing in the door, and my stepfather get to fussing at her. I say, "You can't keep nobody from standing in a door." And he say, "I ain't talking to you." I say, "Just like you is when you talking to my mama." And he might curse at me, and we get to fussing like that.

And they fight about other things. See, both of 'em be drinking. My mother, she don't drink like he do, but she drinks. She don't get drunk much, she get high on the weekend. I don't like my mother to be drunk either. I don't mind her drinking or feeling good, but I don't like for her to get drunk, because she start cursing at him when he says something to her. When she be sober and he says something to her, she don't say nothing; you know, she say, "You don't know what you're talking about."

— Do you remember the maddest you ever got at your stepfather?

That time he cut my mother. I guess I was about eight or nine. I wasn't there but I know they told me that she had got cut. He cut her on the face with a knife. I think she said she was singing a song about she just got some the doctor prescribed for her. And he got mad about it.

— Have you ever wanted to leave home?

Yeah, one time. Me and Bo Dad got to fighting and then I wanted to leave,

I started to leave. I left and went up to one of my cousin's house and stayed up there about two days and I came back home. See, we was standing up to the fireplace and he just walked up to me and slapped me. He had been drinking, you know. Slapped me hard too. And I slapped him back, hard! Hard as I could and we tied up and got to fighting. He tore my dress too. I don't like nobody to tear my clothes.

— Are your mother and stepfather strict?

No. They haven't set down any rules for me. Well, my mother don't like for me to drink on a Sunday night. I have to go to school the next day and I have a hangover and don't want to go.

— What advice have they given you in growing up?

They told me not to, you know, mess up my life. You know, getting pregnant. My mother told me that. And my real daddy, he asked me if I was gon finish school, I said I'm gon try to. He said "You know not to do nothing wrong, don't you?" I said, "Yeah, I'm hip."

— What would you wish for your mother and stepfather if you could make one wish for each that would come true?

I would wish for my mother to get a home of her own. That what she always wants. That's what she says she always wants. She just says she just wants a house of her own.

Betty Brown

And I would get Bo Dad a car. He want one real bad. He always says, "I'm gon get me a car if it's the last thing I do." He says it's hard to get someone to take you to where you want to go if you don't have a car. But if you have a car, you can go where you want to go.

•   •   •

I have one brother and one sister. My brother's eight, my sister's ten. And I had two sisters that died. Both died after they were born. No, my mother didn't have 'em in a hospital, she was at home. Midwives were helping her. I think the older one that died would be about twelve now, going on thirteen. And the baby, she died when we moved to Morgan City, a little community on the other side of town. She'd be about four, I think. She just had been born.

I was in the other room when my mother was having her. My mother, she was crying and grunting. Midwife got there that night, I think. She had the baby the next morning. My stepfather and my stepfather's mother and the midwife and my mother were in the room. In the morning, I asked them if I could come in the room, and they told me I could come in there now. And when I went in there the baby was laying in the bed, and I asked to see it, and Betty told me she was dead.

I was scared at first, but I felt all right afterwards. I hated it, of course. I was frightened, you know, for someone to, you know, die, especially my sister, you know.

— Does your mother ever talk about the babies that died?

My mother never brings it up, not unless somebody bring 'em up, you know. Like they'll ask, "How many children you got?" She'll say, "I had five but I ain't got but three now." She say, "I had two little girls and they died," and then she tell 'em their names. She named 'em. The baby, the last one, was named Debbie Ann Floyd and the first one was named Mary Precious Floyd. She named 'em after they was born. They wasn't dead when they was born, they died after they was born. Long enough for her to name 'em and all that.

— Have you ever thought about the possibility the babies might have lived if they had been born in a hospital?

No.

•   •   •

My first memory was about the time the wind blew down our smokehouse. I must of been 'round about seven, but I was just scared. I was standing out there and the whole house just fell to the side. The wind was blowing very hard!

I had just walked off the back porch. Standing out there. Anyway, the wind blew hard and then the smokehouse fell and I ran in the house. I was crying.

And then I remember the time my uncles got to fighting. I was small. They was fighting over a dollar, I think. My Uncle Arthur owed my Uncle Henry a dollar. Anyway, Henry asked him for it and he wouldn't give it to him, and they got to fighting. And Henry cut Arthur with a knife, he had to go to the hospital. I was in the door, standing in our door. I was crying, I guess I was scared.

My first whipping . . . Oh, I remember one Easter. I don't think I got an Easter dress that year. Me and my cousin, we didn't get an Easter dress that year. Well, anyway, there was a girl that stay next door to us, she got one and she was going to church that Sunday, and we throwed some red mud and hit that dress and my mother whipped us with a switch.

•   •   •

A person I really liked when I was little, well, one of 'em would be my Aunt Ruby. She really my second cousin or something. See, she took care of me when I was sick, good to me, give me things. You know, I used to have rheumatic fever in my legs, and I couldn't walk, and she took care of me. I was about eight. Went on a long time, about two years. You know, I got all right and then I could walk again and then I get back down on my legs and I couldn't walk. I went to school sometimes; you know, when I got all right I went. When I first started getting it, I was staying with my mother, then I got sick and my auntie wanted to keep me, so my mother let me stay with her. Because, you know, she's a good lady and she know what to do. And then I started staying with my grandmother — my father's mother — you know, she wanted to keep me. So I stayed those two years with my aunt and my grandmother.

So about two years ago, my auntie, she was real old and she needed somebody to help her. So I started staying with her. I stayed with her about a year. You know, if I wanted anything she would buy it for me.

•   •   •

My mother's a housemaid. She works for Miss Margaret Jenkins, Shirley McPhee, and Mrs. Redding. Works in the morning time from eight till one. Makes two and a half dollars — fifty cents an hour.

My stepfather is a pulpwood worker. Runs a saw. I don't know how much he makes, probably about sixty dollars a week when it ain't raining, and when it rains he don't work.

— What does he think of his job?

I guess, yeah, he would like a better one. But he don't have any, you know, skills, so he can't get no better one. He hasn't never said he wants a better one, but, you know, he always complain about how he tired of working and he wished he could find him a better job making more money.

— What do you think should be done when someone doesn't have the skills to get a good job?

I don't know, look like there should be sort of like a school, you know, teaching those people who didn't get a chance to get an education to learn something they can do that make more money.

— What does your mother think of her job as a maid?

She often complain about she don't make enough money, she wished that she could get a better job at the mill over here in Howard.

She don't get but fifty cents an hour, and the people she work for give her things sometimes. Christmas and her birthday. Give her money and cigarettes, earrings and necklaces. And sometime when she go to work she bring dresses home, shoes, things for the children to play with. I've gotten dresses from 'em. They was okay dresses, something to wear, you know, but not to really wear out. They was all right.

— Are you satisfied with the clothes you have now?

No, I ain't satisfied with my clothes . . . I would like to have more than what I got. What I got, they look okay. Nothing special. Something special would be real nice clothes, you know, sort of high priced. Most of my dresses are $10.95, $8.95, $7, something like that.

What type would I like to have? Umm, I know one type I would like — how you call it? — it sort of got a design all the way around, you know. All the way around the tail, around the sleeves, around the neck; it's real pretty. I saw it in the store in Columbus. It was white and trim and navy blue, *real* pretty, and I didn't have enough money to get it. I doubt I'll get it very soon.

— Do you consider your family poor?

In a way. We don't have as much as other peoples, and . . . Yeah. We can't afford our own house or a car, we can't afford what we really need, sometimes we can't get it. Like we need something at school, you know, we can get it, but it takes time. I can't get it, you know, when I really need it. Like I need some material in homemaking and I suppose to have it this week, but if my mother don't have any money or I don't get my ten-dollar check from the welfare or a little check from my father, I can't get it. But I probably can get it by the next week or the week after that one. And like one time, we needed some money to pay for our practical English book and I couldn't get it the first week we were supposed to have it. We were suppose to bring the $2.50 that Monday, but I couldn't bring none till that next Monday. I told the teacher that I would bring it when I get it.

— How do you feel about that?

I done got used to it, I guess. A heap of things I need and can't get it when I first need it. I kind of got used to it, I get them later or don't get it at all.

— What do you think of your house?

It's not large enough and it's raggedly, and when it rains, it leaks everywhere, on the beds and everywhere. We need another house. I think about it mostly when we have company. Then I be wishing that we had a better house for them to come in. See, when we first moved over here after our other house got burned up, and peoples came over here, I'd be telling them that we're staying here until we can get a better house, and reason our house not too good because our other one got burned down and we had nowhere else to move. But we've been here about two years.

I hope we can move soon. There's a house on the hill my mother said she was gon try to get. But I don't like up there. It's not a better house but just larger. It's still raggedly, but it's got four rooms and this one don't have but two and there are five of us here. This house only got a kitchen and a front room.

— Where does everyone sleep?

When it's hot, me and my little sister sleep in the kitchen, my little brother sleep in the little cot, and my stepfather and mother sleep together in the front room. And if I have company, like my friend come to stay with me, well, my mother, stepfather, and brother sleep together, my sister sleep in my brother's bed, and me and the company sleep in the kitchen.

And when it's cold, it's real cold in the kitchen because it got more holes in it, so me and my sister sleep in the little bed and my stepfather and mother and brother sleep together.

— Do you ever want more privacy?

Yeah, I want more privacy when I have company. When my boyfriend come to see me I want more privacy but I can't have it. See, my parents, when it's hot, you know, they go out in the kitchen, but when it cold they'll stay in the front room by the fireplace where we are. See, the house be real cold in the winter. Like you be over to the fire, your legs be burning up and your back be freezing.

— Where do you get water?

We get our water out of the water pipe outside. Yeah, I would like for us to have inside water, but since we never had any it don't bother me. If we had

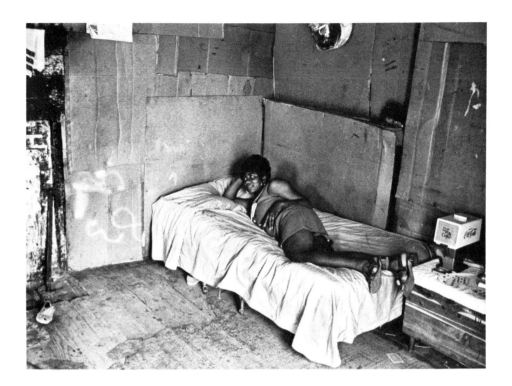

water inside of the house I guess we would have a bathroom and a bathtub. You wouldn't have to worry about at night emptying the water out after we take a bath, and always going out in the cold getting water when it be raining. See, I bathe in the kitchen in a tub. Get the water out of the pipe and put it in a pan and heat it on the stove and pour it in the tub. I used to could sit down in it when I was small, but I can't now. You know, I sort of sit on the rim of it.

Yeah, I'd like a bathtub, and I would like a bathroom. You know, the stool, so, you know, so I wouldn't have to go outside and use the bathroom. I don't like to go out there. I won't go out there when it be cold, I use the pot in the house and then I take it out. You call it the slop jar. Anyway, it be outdoors and then I go get it and bring it in the house and use it in the closet — you don't have much space — and I take it back outdoors and wash it out.

— Of the things you have said you don't like about your house, which is the worst?

What about all of 'em? See, I would like to have more privacy but I *would* like for it to be warm in the house and when it get cold I *would* like to use the bathroom inside the house and not have to go outside and then I would like it if I didn't have to heat my water to take a bath.

Betty Brown

We pay fifteen dollars a month rent. The man who own the house don't never repair it. I think they told him about the leaking in the roof, but he didn't never do nothing about it. I think he ought to fix it because it's his house and we pay rent and if we didn't have to pay no rent, if we owned it, we would fix it up. It would be ours and then he couldn't put us out soon as we get it fixed.

See, I think he done talked about putting us out. When Bo Dad get drunk, you know, he sort of raise sand. I think he be disturbing the peoples and they said something to Mr. Eddie Spencer about it and Mr. Spencer told him the other day that if he didn't do better, that we were gon have to move.

— What's the difference between the house of the average white and the house of the average Negro around here?

Well, the white people's houses are better than the Negro houses. Negro houses are raggedly. Wood houses. Raggedly inside, rain in them. White people's houses are good, don't none of 'em hardly rain inside that I know of. Painted. Most of them not wood houses either. Brick.

•　　•　　•

— Do your parents ever talk about being poor?

My parents have just said they wish they had more money, you know, to buy what they wanted. And they wish they could buy us more. That's all they say. Like if I tell my mother I want a new dress, she'll say, "Child, I ain't got no money to buy you no dress with. You know I got to get Donna a dress to go on her chapel program." And I said, "You don't never hardly buy me nothing." She said, "I don't have money, child, you know I ain't hardly got no money, you know I don't have much money and I buy you what I can." I say okay.

· · ·

If I had a million dollars, I'd buy me a wardrobe. Then I'd give my mother some.
— What right now do you feel you *need* the most?
A record player. I like to listen at music and I ain't got nary'n. I had one but the man took it back. My stepfather got it. But he didn't pay the payments on it. The payments were too high for me to pay so the man got it back. He came to the house. I didn't want him to take it. But there wasn't nothing I could do because I couldn't pay the payments.

· · ·

— Have you ever thought that one day you might have a good bit of money?
Yeah. Yeah, that one reason I want to finish school, so I can get a better job than my people got. Then I can help them. After they get old they ain't gon be able to do no work, you know, hard work like they doing now.
I don't care what kind of job I get. After I finish school I just wanna go up the country and get a good job. I never really thought about what kind of job I'd try to get.
— Do you think you will get one making good money?
Sure! I expect to get one making good money. Maybe close to a hundred dollars a week, I'd call that good money.
— Can you think of anything that could keep you from getting a good job? No.
— Have your parents ever said what they'd like you to do?
My father, my real one, mentioned once that he wanted me to go to college and become a teacher so I could take care of my old man. My mother never said anything about it. She said whatever you wanna do when you finish school, that's okay. I said, "I probably go up the country to Boston and get a good job. So I can sort of pay you off for, you know, what you did for me." She said, "You never be able to repay me for what I done did for you." You know, that's all she said. I said, "Maybe I be able to help you in some way." She said, "Probably so."
Yeah, I told her I'd go to Boston. My Uncle Stewart, he says it's a very

lovely place, and I want to see it. He just said it's a big place, and you have a lot of places to go, that he have a good time, and I'm crazy about a good time. And it's not no work around here. Shoot, you can get a better job up there because it's larger and there are many more peoples to work for.

I think I'd like the city better than the country, like where I'm living now. There are more places to go than it is in the country. Make more money in the city than you do in the country. You can get a better place to live in the city than you can in the country. You know, when you go out in the city, you'll learn how to act, but most of the peoples in the country, they don't know how to act. They act different, you know. Like they ain't used to being nowhere or doing nothing.

•   •   •

I pray just about every night. I say the Lord's Prayer, then I ask God to forgive me for the sins I have committed that day, and I ask him to take care of the peoples that are going out for the sake of his name, and I ask him to take care of my family and help 'em and direct 'em to go the right way and to help the sick peoples. I say 'em to myself when I get into the bed, but my mother, you know, she get down on the floor on a chair on her knees and say it every night.

— Do you ever ask God for anything?

It probably stupid, but I remember one time I asked God to help me forget about a boy. I just asked Him to release the feelings that I had for him from my heart. We had broke up and he was with another girl. I didn't want to like him anymore, but I did. And I ask Him to help me get a new dress.

•   •   •

I don't like school. I don't like to go. I don't like getting up in the morning time. I don't like a teacher. My home economics teacher. She mean. She talk about people. She just mean. You know, like a girl had on a summer dress when it was cold, and she made her get out there in front of the class, and she talked about her. She said, "You know better than wear a dress like that to school, as cold as it is, you going be done caught the pneumonia." You know, everybody laughed at her, I'm sure she was embarrassed. But I didn't laugh. And then Rebecca, this other girl, she had a low-cut dress, come right here, you know, you could see this here part, you know, at the bust. The teacher said she shouldn't be wearing a dress like that to school. She said now if a boy was to say something to her, she couldn't get mad with him because she's just showing it all to him anyway.

And they whip you in school. Like last year, Mrs. Donaldson was gon whip me and some more girls, I think we had gone out of the room or something. Anyway, the lady that was our basketball coach last year had just tore us up a couple of days before. We were bruised! You know, the basketball coach had whipped us bad. And so I said, "Mrs. Donaldson, you can't whip me because I'm bruised where the coach whipped me." I said, "I've been to the doctor." But I hadn't really. That's what kept me from getting down on that floor on my knees.

See, our basketball coach, I'll tell you, that lady liked to kilt me. We were winning all the games, every game we played we were winning. And we played Butler and we lost and our coach said we didn't do nothing. She said we didn't try. So we was eighteen points behind and she gave us eighteen licks apiece with a paddle. Gave everybody eighteen licks, even the ones that didn't play.

The meanest teacher I ever had? Mrs. Herd. She kept her nose in the air. And she was mean, she was real mean. She'd whip you. I stayed out of school that day she was gon whip the whole class. Nobody had their lessons. Gave everybody an F and was still gon whip 'em. And she whipped 'em, but she didn't whip me because I stayed at home. And one day she said she gon whip us I think I wore about ten pair of stockings to school. She didn't whip us that day. But she had a strap. She'd whip you on your legs and whip you 'cross your back.

— Do you study much?

Sometimes I study, not too much. I make A's and B's and C's, mostly A's and B's.

— Do you ever miss school?

I missed last Monday, I had a bad hangover. Got high the night before. I wish I could of missed this Monday. I stayed in the clinic all day. We was just drinking and dancing the night before. Boy, my head liked to kill me. I got put out of homemaking and I went to the clinic and slept all day long. See, our home economics teacher, she was showing a film about how your breakfast is the best part. And so this girl in the film named BJ. So she was a breakfast jumper, you know; she didn't never eat breakfast. So my home economics teacher said, "All these breakfast jumpers, their skin look like they're about dirty." You know, I was sitting right behind her, and I said, "I feel like I'm about dirty." You know, everything the teacher said, I had something to match it. Well, anyway, she told me I may be excused, you know, and I went to the clinic. Next day she sent for me, she said she knew I had a hangover and she said I could come back to class.

— Do you plan to finish school?

Yeah, mostly because my mama want me to. She just said she want me to do one thing in my life. I said, "What is that?" She said, "I want you to finish school." I said, "Okay, I'll finish. At least I'll give it a good try." I guess she want me to have what she didn't have. She didn't get no further than the eighth grade. And I just wanna finish. I wanna finish myself, so I can get a good job. It's hard to get a job if you don't have an education. And if you don't have a job, you won't be getting no money, and you can't live without money. Not too good.

— Would you like to go to college?

No, I wouldn't like to go to college. Twelve years of school is enough for me!

— If someone offered you a scholarship, would you go?

Yeah, I'd go then.

— So if you had the money, you'd go?

I don't know, I don't think so. I don't like school no way.

— Well, why would you go if someone offered you a scholarship?

Because I'd have the chance to become something. But if it was free to go, just like it free to go to school, I wouldn't go. But if someone was to give me a scholarship, I'd go. Because they gave it to me.

• • •

What do I do for fun? I play basketball. Crazy about that. I like that better'n anything. I made captain this year. In the seventh grade after a game at night, the principal would let the students play. I played like that when I was in the seventh grade, and when I got in the eighth grade I went out for the team. I made first string the first year. And the next year — that's this year — I made captain. I was very excited. My first thought was, I must can play pretty good, they made me captain. And this year in the tournament we got second place and went to the semi-finals. This year, Carver girls got farther than they ever went. The Tigerettes.

And I like to go to Columbus and go to drive-ins. But I don't go too often. Like since this year came in, I haven't been but twice. I like the sexy pictures. I like to see what's happening, I guess. My favorite movie star is . . . I don't know, I used to like Marilyn Monroe. I liked the way she act and how she be talking. I think she cute.

I saw the one *Hot Rods to Hell,* that was a really good one. It was a lot of teen-agers, you know, sort of living in a world to theirself, and they was ruling it. And I liked how they dancing and the clothes that they wore and the cars that they were driving; I like to ride fast and they were driving fast. They didn't have nobody to tell them what to do or when to come home and stop doing it, you know. They just did it as long as they wanted to and came home when they got ready.

There's actually nothing too much to do around here. On the weekends, just go out to the grill mostly. Mostly just teen-agers go there. You just sit at the tables and eat, and if you want to you can play some music and get up and dance. I like to go out there because all my friends be out there, and that's a good place to be with your boyfriend. Just about everybody that go there I know 'em. And sometimes I go to a club in Daisy called the Proud Ace and a place over there called Bubble Flowers. And we go to Bartlett, at Norman's Place.

— What's the most enjoyable evening you have had at the grill?

It was one Friday night. All my friends was out there, my boyfriend was out there, everybody was dancing and drinking and I liked that. Didn't nobody get to fighting. Usually somebody gets to fighting and we have to leave early, you know, before the lady gon call the police. Didn't nobody get into it that night and we stayed there a long time.

See, sometimes boys get to fighting about girls, you know. Like a boy be going with a girl and another boy be dancing with her and he try to break and the boy won't let him and they probably get to fighting about that. Or somebody step on somebody's toe, different things. The boys, they have sticks, pieces of iron, tote knives, and pistols. Lots of 'em have pistols, and they be shooting.

Like last weekend. These boys were fighting, hitting each other. And these other two boys, they were shooting. One was just shooting in the air and the other one was shooting down at the ground, trying to stop those other boys from fighting. And one of the boys that was shooting left and he gave Cathy the pistol because they was gon call the police. And I got the pistol from Cathy and then I shot. I think I pulled it twice. It shot once and snapped once and I gave it back to them. I was trying to stop them from fighting but they weren't paying no attention.

I got to fussing with a couple of girls out there recently. About a boy. This here boy, he goes with both of us, me and this other girl. Anyway, it was late and I never had got out to the grill — it was about ten o'clock — I just had came from Columbus. And when I got out to the grill I saw this boy — he got a baby by this other girl, too. Anyway, he was sitting over at a table with her, and I went over there and I hit on the table and I say, "Hi, hi everybody." Everybody say hi and he say hi real low. I said, "The cat must got your tongue." He didn't say nothing. I say, "The cat got your tongue?" And he said, "Yeah!" And when he said that, that girl what he got the baby by, she slapped him. And then I slapped him, she slapped him, I slapped him, and then he jump up and went out and then this girl's cousin said, "Let me by." And I wouldn't move, she shoved me and I shoved her back. And she told me to come outdoors, that she been wanting to whip me a long time. And I went outdoors and me and her got to fussing. She didn't do nothing though.

— What's the most hell-raising night you've ever had?

During the summer when me and Cathy went to Daisy to the club. Well, we went with two boys and when we got there, there was a band over there, and so we was just dancing with most all the boys and having a good time drinking. We just met a lot of boys and they bought us a lot to drink and we were dancing with them and they got to fussing about us. And then our boyfriends came out there to Daisy and they got mad with us because we were with those boys. And then they got with some more girls, but we didn't care because we was having a good time. But, anyway, we got with the boys we came with and came back home. And when we got back home our boyfriends were here, up to Cathy's house. I went up there. We got into it.

When we walked into the house, you know, we was sort of scared, and we went where Cathy's mama were. Then they came in there and snatched us and slapped us and I ran into the kitchen. My boyfriend came in there with a pistol, telling me he was gon kill me, but there wasn't nothing in it. He snapped it and there wasn't nothing in it. And then I ran back out the door, he was behind me. Then everything got all right.

•   •   •

I have four real good friends, or at least I did. Sharon Ann Parker, Barbara Johnson, Vera Hodges, and Cathy Smith. Two of 'em, Barbara and Vera, go to school, and two of 'em, Sharon Ann and Cathy, don't. I guess the two that don't go to school, they are really my *best* friends. You know, I'll mostly be out with them on the weekend. We like the same things. I like to have fun, I like to go out, I like to talk about my boyfriend, sometimes I like to talk and not get lessons.

They dropped out of school. They got pregnant. See, you have to drop out when you get pregnant. One got pregnant when she was fifteen and the other, I don't know how old she was, but she dropped out in the seventh grade.

— How did they feel about getting pregnant?

They say they hated it when they got pregnant. I guess they wanted to finish school. And Sharon Ann says if she gets pregnant again, she's gon kill herself. But after they got pregnant, they wanted to have their baby. They seem to love their babies. They hate they messed up in life, but since they have, they don't regret it. Both of 'em stay with their parents. Sharon Ann, she get a check from the welfare, and Cathy, she get one too. Cathy, she's married, her husband on the gang. I think he tried to burn up their house or something and kill 'em, I'm not for sure.

I was gon tell you about Sharon Ann and Cathy. Actually, Cathy used to be my real good friend, but she ain't really now. And Sharon Ann, well, I don't guess she is now. See, they got mad at me about something they did . . . and Barbara and me didn't do it. See, last Thursday we went to the club in Columbus with some mens, some boys, at the Club Lavanna. Well, see, we ain't never seen these boys before. Anyway, they set up the table and put plenty of liquor — as much liquor as I have ever seen in my life — on the table and beer and stuff. So I didn't drink much because I had to go to school and I just had been put out of homemaking that Monday for being drunk. I said I wasn't gon drink nothing, and Barbara, she was gon stay with me, you know. So Cathy and Sharon Ann started drinking — I told 'em not to drink much. Every time the boys asked me to dance, I wouldn't dance with 'em, so they called me a square. And I called her into the bathroom and told her not to drink much because they didn't know nothing 'bout them boys. But they wouldn't listen to me.

Anyway, Sharon Ann and Cathy left with two of those mens. And me and Barbara, we left and came on back home. That was Thursday night and they didn't get back home until that Friday night. Sure didn't. Well, anyway, their mothers came up here and asked me where they were, so I told 'em. But, you know, everybody was saying something about 'em, but Barbara and I, everything somebody say we'll take up for 'em, you know. And when they got back home, I guess they figured we had said something about 'em, you know, since they left with these mens and we didn't. But I hadn't said nothing! And so I went up there and told 'em that I hadn't said nothing about it. Anyway, I guess they was sort of mad at us about that.

Anyway, I went out to the grill Friday night. And Sharon Ann's sister was there. She named Lenora, she married, been married about four times, she still sort of young. I don't guess she act like she got good sense. She been in a lot of fights because she got some cuts on her face.

Anyway, I was out there by myself. And I went in the bathroom, and Lenora came in. Lenora said, "You and Sharon Ann were very good friends before you started going out with Barbara, wasn't you?" I said, "Yeah . . ." Then she said, "Well, if you gon be Barbara's friend, you just can't be Sharon Ann's friend." I said, "Well, I just won't be Sharon Ann's friend then."

You know, she got a quick temper, she got mad just like that and went out. So I went on out too, behind her. And I started dancing and she was sitting at a table. She had a knife in her pocketbook, I had a razor in my bosom. So she was just looking at me, rolling her eyes, when I was dancing, and I quit dancing. So I went over there, I said, "Something the matter with your eyes?" Then she said, "Ain't nothing the matter with my eyes." I said, "How come you rolling them at me then?" And me and her got to fussing.

You know Sharon Ann got a baby, and she said, "Well, you the cause of Sharon Ann got that damned baby down there." And when she said that I slapped her. So then she went in the bathroom and I went in behind her. And then I said, "How come you don't like me, Lenora?" And then she said, "How come you don't like me?"

And then me and her got to fighting; I jacked up in a corner when she said that, and then we were fighting. She scratched me, but I scratched her back, honey! And then after they stopped us from fighting, you know, and she was standing up there talking, it was a heap of people around her, and it was a heap of 'em around me. She had pulled her knife out then. And I took my razor out and then I cut at her, I cut her right across her sleeve. And then she said, "Oh hell! This son of a bitch done cut me." But I hadn't cut her. Then she said, "No, she ain't, she just cut my sleeve." So I put my razor back down in my bosom right quick. And then she was coming up on me with her knife, you know, and I was backing back off. You know, I was trying to get my razor out and about that time Pat and Johnny had throwed her down and took her knife.

I didn't cut her, I was trying to cut her though. Yeah, trying to slice her to death. I wished I had of got to her, too.

Oh! . . . Saturday night Bo Dad, my stepfather, got messed up out there. Jim Baker shot at him four times. He's a big old man, he kicked Bo Dad all in the face, knocked him out. And shot four times, two in the place and two out. I don't know what they were arguing about. I know Bo Dad had a razor, both of 'em had a razor. I think Bo Dad tried to use his razor.

When Bo Dad got in that fight out to the grill, I was helping him. He sort of thought that I didn't like him, but I guess I proved to him I liked him, so we pretty good friends now. You know, he was laying out there on the ground and I picked him up and me and his sister got somebody to take him home and then I tried to talk to him. And then I went back there to the grill and I talked to the guy who kicked him and he said he didn't do it. But he did do it. Me and him got to fussing.

•　　•　　•

I was about thirteen when boys really started taking me out. See, I used to go out with my aunt when I was eleven or twelve. Used to stay with her on weekends; she was nineteen or twenty. We went out and just went to clubs and parties and things like that. So you can say I started real young, which I did. I got hip. See, I look older than my age and when I got old enough to know what was going on, boys taking me out, I knew about these clubs and cafés and wild parties and things, where drinking and fighting going on. Mother got me to stop going to spend the night with my aunt.

When I was twelve, going on thirteen, I had some girls who was my close friends. And a heap of boys used to come see us at the same time. But mainly two. They used to be sitting on the porch and they both put their arms around me and said which one do you want. I said both.

But the nicest one, I didn't like him as much as I did the bad one. I don't know why. The bad one, he didn't look no better or nothing like that. He talked bad. You know, he be asking me when you gon do something. He said, "I been

coming down here a long time and still you ain't done nothing." Nice one didn't never say nothing about a relationship, you know.

Now I got two boyfriends, I did have two. I ain't got but one now. See, that one that I was telling you about what got the baby by another girl, the one I slapped at the grill the other night when he was out there with her, he ain't my boyfriend no more. I was gon quit him anyway. I'm sure I could start back going with him if I wanted to, but I don't want to. Because of that girl.

I'd been going with him for about a year. I liked him because he like to have a good time and I like that. Because he have a car and I like to ride. I don't know why else. I guess I wanted somebody who already had somebody, see could I take 'em. That's mainly the reason.

Yeah, I like to do that. I don't know why, I get a kick out of it. I guess I be able to say I took him from her, but I can't say that this time.

— Have you taken many boys away from other girls?

Yeah, I've taken away a right smart of 'em. Like one time, you know, I was young . . . you know how school children have crushes on boys. Well, anyway, this girl, she was going with a boy — been going with him for a long time — and then he started liking me. You know, I wasn't receiving any company then. I was about twelve. But, you know, I always been big for my age, I guess he thought I was about fourteen. Anyway, we was coming from the schoolhouse one night — I knew he was going with a girl, you know — and so he was walking with me and she came up there and grabbed him and she said, "You got to make up your mind right now who you want." Then he said, "I ain't with you, Ethel." And then she said, "What you mean?" And he said, "I'm with who I want." And so that was it.

When I was in the sixth grade, I took a boy from my best friend. She used to talk about him *all* the time; she say, "I know I got him, can't nobody take him." I said, "I'm gon get him, watch and see." And then that summer we out of school, and he used to come around all the time; I be messing with him. And then finally he started liking me, I guess. Then when school started back that next year, me and my friend were still friends. I said, "I told you I was gon get that boy." She said, "Huh-uh, I still got him." I said, "No, you ain't; watch him take me to the game." He came and took me to the game, and she got mad with me.

— Have you ever gone out with any married men?

Wanna know the truth? Yeah. One. In '68 and '69. I went out with him a lot to Bartlett to the club. I liked him about the same as the others. He was about twenty-something.

— Did you know his wife?

Yeah, I knew his wife. I know her name, I don't know her that good. She found out about it about nine months after I started going with him. I had been seeing him for nine months before she found out about it. They got to fighting, but he kept going out with me. She didn't say anything to me, she just looked at me strange when she saw me. We see each other on the streets sometimes now.

What did I think about going out with him? I didn't think it was no different at first. And then I found out that I shouldn't of been going out with him. Because a married man don't mean a young girl no good. He couldn't because he ain't got no future with her; he already got a wife. And really he'll just be trying to have a good time, you know, because he got something to go back home to. I saw this after we had broken up.

Betty Brown

My mother had told me, you know. She didn't approve of it at all. She told me to quit seeing him. I said okay. But I didn't, not then no way. So she said, "I told you, Tiny" — that's what she calls me — "to leave him alone." I said, "I'm gon leave him alone. It take time, I don't want to just come out and tell him." And we would get to arguing about it. She said, "You ain't got no business going with him." I said, "I told you I was gon quit seeing him." She said, "I hope you telling the truth because it's for your own good." I said, "I'm telling the truth, I ain't got no reason to tell no story."

— Did you get mad at her?

Yeah, I got mad at her. When she said he was ugly, and I knew he was cute, I got mad about that. Because he wasn't ugly a'tall.

— Do you think you treat boys right?

No, I try to but I always mess up in some way. Like these boys, if you going with them, they don't want you to go with others. Like I'm going with Don, and Sue and Eugene and Joe come over and want me to go to the club, and I just go. I think that I really like 'em, but I must not or I'd stay at home. But when I'm with 'em, I really like 'em.

— Do you think it will be the same way with your husband if you get married?

No, I'm gon be true to my husband, but until I marry though . . . ! !

— What kind of person would you like to marry?

I want him to be sort of tall, you know, just a little taller than I am so I'll have to reach up to kiss him, and I want him to be sweet and very considerate, very conversational and have good manners, very respectable — you know, don't curse and get drunk and fight. You know, I don't mind him drinking to have a good time and at special occasions but just every day . . . I don't want him to do that. I don't like for nobody to do it. It's ugly, make 'em look stupid. And I want him to have a light complexion and I want him to be sort of cute.

— Why a light complexion?

I don't know why I want him to have a light complexion. All I know I do. I sort of like light-colored folks better. And I wouldn't want him to spend all his money on liquor. And not just want for himself but want for his family.

— What kind of person do you think you'll end up marrying?

I don't know, I might wind up marrying Mickey. This is the boyfriend I was telling you about, the one I got now. Not the one I slapped the other night, the other one. He about nineteen, twenty, twenty-one. We talk about getting married sometime. He just say he want to marry me when I finish school. And I say okay. And he say, "Don't be playing with me, it ain't nothing to play with." I say, "I ain't kidding; for real, I wanna marry you." You know, we talk about things like that.

And when he heard I was going with that other boy, he said, "You know, you sure is messing up fast. I thought you wanted me to wait on you." I said, "Now, if you wanna wait on me . . ." He said, "Yeah, you know I wanna wait on you but you messing up . . ." Then I said, "I ain't doing nothing." I said, "You ain't seen me do nothing." Then he said, "Just like I seen you." And I said, "No, it ain't. I ain't did nothing." But you know I done did something.

— Do you think you'll make a good wife?

Uh-huh. Because I'll be good to my husband, and cook for him and clean for him, and I'll stay home with the children and take good care of them. That's all that's required for a good wife, don't it?

— Do you want to have a family?

Yeah, I'd wanna have a family about three years after I got married. I want to get a place for us to stay, get settled, and probably through paying for our furniture before, and I wanna live in a trailer. I always wanted to live in a trailer.

I'd want about one child. That's because it's hard to have a baby, and if I have to go through all those pains the first time, I ain't gon wanna go through 'em no more. I saw my aunt have a baby when I was about eleven. She had it in our house, she was staying with us. Well, everybody was in there. You know, my father and mother and sister and brother, they was in the other room looking at TV. I was in there too. And Little Sister — that's what they call my aunt — she was in her room. You know, she was pregnant and she kept walking around in the room holding her stomach. I run in there, I said, "What's the matter with you, fixing to have your baby?" And she said, "Get out of here!" And I went in and told my mother about it, that she was holding her stomach, and then she went in there.

And then that night she started crying. You know, she was hollering out, talking about "Oh Lord, oh help me" and all that. Then she got down on the floor on a pallet right by the stove and she had her head on it and, you know, she was sort of wide-legged. And my stepdaddy, he was gone for the midwife then, but she hadn't got there. My aunt was crying, they were rubbing her stomach. And . . . it just happened.

See, we was peeping in the door, and after they saw us peeping, they run us out. And after they saw we had saw everything, they just let us come on in. Then they put the baby on the floor on a pallet; you know, they hadn't cleaned her up then and they laid something over her and the midwife got there, bathed her.

— Is that the only reason you want only one baby?

I don't want but one little girl no way.

— Why?

Because you can dress 'em pretty. And, you know, children just take up so much responsibility and money, you know. I don't want but one so I can get her just about everything she wants.

Yeah, I think I'd be a good mother. Whip their butt though if they didn't mind. Tear 'em up! If you don't get 'em to mind you when they little, they sure won't mind you when they big.

— Would you raise your children differently than you were raised?

Yeah, I'd try to. I wouldn't let 'em be around so much cussing, I make people respect them as children. Not saying everything around 'em. About what grown people done did and a heap of things. Like this man done been with this man's wife and he come back talking about it.

· · ·

Do I think women need men? Huh-uh, not necessarily. I could make it without one myself.

— All through life?

I don't know, but I'll give it a good try. I've thought about it. Shoot, I don't need no husband. I don't think I ever wanna marry nobody. I can rent me an apartment myself and go to work and furnish it. Being married tie you down, you know, you can't go when you wanna and come back when you get ready.

I like single life. See, when I'm not married I know what I have. But when I'm married I won't know what I'm going to have. Like if I be single — and, you know, after I finish school and go out in the world on my own and have my own apartment and a little furniture, you know, and just enough money to buy me something with, well, I know I have that. But if I marry I won't know what I'm gon have. I might lose what I got and still not gain anything.

· · ·

Not too many Negroes around here like white people. But they shouldn't hate all white people, because all white peoples aren't bad. Some of 'em is, though, just about the majority of 'em. They is. It's some nice white peoples around here and some of 'em around here is bad and some of 'em, I don't know whether they nice or bad. Some of 'em treats colored peoples very cruel. Like they holler at 'em for nothing when they be trying to talk nice to them.

I remember one time this colored person was at our house. And Mr. Joe, this white man that the colored man owed money to, he passed by here, said, "Is Frank here?" I said, "Yeah." So I came in the house and told Frank — that's the colored man — and he said, "You shouldn't have told him I was here." I said, "Too bad now, I done told him." So the colored man told Mr. Joe that he didn't have any money to pay him, and Mr. Joe told him if he didn't pay him his damn money both of 'em couldn't live in Adamsville. Said he'd bring his blackjack around here.

And I don't like Mrs. Farmer! No, good gracious! She work at this clothes store uptown, and you go in there for something . . .

"Can I help you?"

"We just looking."

"Well, you done looked a hundred times at these things! You know what we got in, we ain't got nothing new." You know, she sort of embarrass you, you know. Heap of people be in there, you know. I said, "Well, I wanna look again then." She say, "Well, I ain't got all day for you to just be looking." I say, "Probably I wanna buy something, I got to look first." She was hollering, so I hollered back at her — naturally. Because if she figured I was a dog for her to holler at, I figured she was one, I could holler back at her.

— Have you ever gotten so mad at a white person that you felt like hitting him?

No, I haven't. But I'll hit them if they hit me.

— Have you ever been called a nigger?

One time we was going to town, it was some little white boys in a car, they holler out the window and said, "Niii-ger." Sure did. I didn't say nothing, they just jetted by, you know — "Nigger." I didn't like it. My friend cursed, I didn't say nothing. I just did like that [shrugged her shoulders] and kept going.

— What do you think of whites who want to hold Negroes down?

I don't like those kind of peoples.

— Tell me about some.

Eisenhower did one time, didn't he? Yep, wanted to hold Negroes down. Wasn't he running for president one time? Uh-huh, he didn't make it either, did he? I don't know if it was true but I heard some people saying that he said that he was gon try to get Negroes back in slavery time. I said to myself, He'll *never* make president. Never! !

— What changes would you like to see in the majority of white people?

For the colored to have just as much as whites.

— Do you think it will happen?

Yeah. I don't know when, it might happen sooner than I think.

I'm Somebody Important   32

— How will it happen?

Easy. Just like they got the advance, colored people might get it. I don't know how. Colored peoples is pretty smart, they get smarter and smarter every day, they'll think of a way, I'm sure. In a heap of ways they getting smarter. Figuring out how to do better things, figuring out how to get things, how to run businesses. A lot of colored people can do things better than white, or just as good. Plenty of things — run a business, be the boss of a company, heap of things.

— What do you think about whites having more money than Negroes?

I don't know, I don't think nothing about it, but they is got more money than Negroes have.

— Is that okay with you?

No, I don't like it. There ain't nothing I can do about it though.

— Do you dislike it?

No, because it they money. I wished I had some of it though. But there are some poor white people too. You know that? I never did have no idea why some white people had more than others. I thought once because probably they came from a more wealthier family than others, but some white peoples can be related and some still be poorer than others. There are some poor white people, sure are.

— Do you know any Negroes who work in offices?

Huh-uh. All I know is they pulp wood, work on telephone poles or the railroad, put up fences or something. They ain't got no skill, they got to do something to make a living.

— What's more important, having respect as a person or having a nice house and a lot of money?

And not having respect as a person? Having respect as a person. I just prefer that. Bad as I would like to have money and things, if I had a choice, I believe I'd take respect as a person.

— Will you tell your children anything about race?

Sure, I'll tell 'em about how a Negro used to couldn't go in front of a place — by the time I have children I'm sure they'll be able to go in the front by then. I tell 'em about how they used to couldn't and about after they passed the law that they could, they still couldn't go in all places. You know, it's still some bathrooms that can't nobody go in but white peoples. Everywhere they got those for white only.

— Do you think it's wrong for restaurants and other places to be segregated?

Yeah, because they don't supposed to be like that. But if I be hungry and pass by there, I go in the side and get me something to eat.

Betty Brown

— How do you feel about going in the side instead of the front?

Well, I ain't thought too much about it, but I don't supposed to be going in the side, I suppose to be going in the front. But I'd go in the side to get a hamburger; I wouldn't think nothing about it.

No, the side part ain't as nice as the front in this restaurant up here. I never been in the front, but I looked in there through the window. It's nicer than the side part. The tables are better, the chairs, the floors aren't the same.

— Do you have any feelings about having to eat in the side while the front is nicer?

Huh-uh, I haven't thought nothing about it. But you *supposed* to be able to go in the front. But you can't go in the front of all of 'em, we can't. Well, there was a man here from Atlanta Sunday visiting us, and me and my aunt went out to the grill with him. He was gon get something to eat and it was closed and we was going to stop back at this other restaurant, and I told him we couldn't go in the front, you know, we had to go in the side. Well, *he* would have gone in the front if I'd of showed him where to stop. He said he was going in the front because we supposed to go in the front. But I didn't show him where to stop.

See, my aunt didn't want me to tell him. She told me not to tell him because she didn't want him to go in there if they didn't want us to go in there. But he said that we don't supposed to go in the back or the side anymore. If it's a front door, if white people go in the front door, we supposed to be able to go in the front too. And he said he was going in there and wasn't nobody gon bother him. And my aunt told me not to show him where the place is. And I didn't. When we got to the place, he said, "Is this the place?" I said, "Huh-uh, this not the place, it down a little farther." And then we got down in town, he said, "Where the place at?" I said, "Let me out," and I got out.

— Would you have told him if it weren't for your aunt?

If my aunt hadn't told me not to tell him where it was, I would of told him. I wanted to see what they gon say in the restaurant. I would of gone in with him. I sure would. I wanted to see what they were gon say and how they were gon react and what he was gon say and how he was gon react.

— Are there any white students at your school?

No. They could come if they wanted to, but I don't guess they want to. They probably like their own school; I like my own school, I wouldn't go to theirs unless I had to. I wouldn't want to. I just wouldn't like to go to their school because I know everybody at my school, you know, and I wouldn't know everybody if I was to go over there. I just don't think I would like their school.

I don't wanna go over there! I guess if Vera and Barbara went, I'd wanna go.

— What if half of the white students were transferred to your school and half of the black students were transferred over there?

Would I like that? Huh-uh. I just wouldn't, I don't know why. Huh-uh, I *know* I wouldn't like it.

— Did you have any white playmates when you were little?

Yeah, I used to have one white girl I played with, Mary Jordan. When I was small my mother used to work for her mother and she used to take me to work with her, and we used to play together. I liked her, very much! She was nice.

But we don't do nothing together now. We just speak. She ask me how I be doing, I tell her all right, ask about her family, see if they doing okay, go on about my business.

— Have you ever been jealous of white girls for having more clothes and living in a better house?

No. I always wished I live in a nice house and had a lot of clothes, but I never been jealous. See, when I saw them with nicer clothes on, I didn't get mad because they had it, and I didn't get mad when I saw them living in a better house than I did. I just wished that I was living there. But because I wasn't and they were, I didn't get mad with 'em about it.

— How do you think you would react if all of a sudden you found yourself in the environment of an average white person?

Just like a white person? I would like that. I don't know how I would react, but I would like it, I know that. Especially living in a fine house and all the clothes. It don't matter to me about whether we go in the side of a restaurant or in the front. Just as long as I'm going in and getting what I want, I don't care. I don't; it might be stupid, but I don't.

— Do you think the races will ever get together?

Yeah. I don't know how it will happen, but I believe it will happen, sooner or later. I guess I just got hope, faith.

•　　•　　•

I guess all government officials are white because whites have advantages over Negroes in many ways, and that's one of the ways. I don't know how they got the advantages, but I guess it because Negroes were in slavery and they was the boss over 'em. Most of 'em still want to be the boss over 'em, but . . . they ain't.

— What do you think about how the government is run?

It's run good. It seem to be helping people that need help — you know, like giving out free food and giving the poor money, welfare. We get the free food.

— Do you think it is doing enough?

No, they ain't fixing up these raggedly houses.

— Do you believe anyone powerful around here cares about poor people?

No, they don't act like it. They ain't doing nothing about it. They should, you know, talk to the government away up there and help us get better places to live. It rains in these houses, just like they outdoors.

.   .   .

— What did you think about Dr. Martin Luther King?

I think he was a good man. He *got* Negroes in a better position than they were at first, and he would of got 'em in a better position than that if they hadn't killed him. I think so.

— How did you feel when he was killed?

I'm Somebody Important

Just like I do now. I hated it, you know, but there wasn't no strings attached to it. I mean it didn't bother me. I hated it he was dead, but it didn't bother me.

— Who would you say was the better leader, King or President Nixon?

I would say Martin Luther King. Because he was a Negro. Sure would. You want to know the truth, don't you?

— Have you ever heard of Malcolm X?

No, who was he?

— He was a militant and sometimes suggested that if changes were not made, there should be violence.

Well, he should still be living then. Somebody else done took his place? Or they just let the organization drop?

— Do you think there should be violence?

No, no. If they don't change it, then . . . It need to be changes. But I don't know about the violence, I don't like violence too much. But if that's the only way gon get change, it's okay. But some of that violence ain't getting 'em nowhere. Getting people hurt.

— Have you ever heard of Julian Bond?

No. Who was he?

— He is a black member of the Georgia House, and his name was placed for nomination for vice-president, but he wasn't old enough.

I don't think he would have made it and don't even know him. I think it be a long time before a Negro become vice-president or president. No white peoples would vote for a Negro. They just wouldn't. None of 'em. Would you?

— Have you ever heard of the NAACP, the Urban League, the SCLC, or the Black Panthers?

No, I haven't heard of any of those.

— Would you like there to be a civil rights organization here?

I don't know, it wouldn't make no difference to me if there were.

— If a store here would not hire Negroes and someone staged an economic boycott, would you shop at that store?

They did that at Penney's in Columbus. You know, I was going in the store and it was some Negro peoples out there, you know, men. And they gave me a piece of paper and I read that and they told me don't shop at Penney's because they won't hire no Negroes, and they said they don't want no black peoples to work there, they just want black money. And the Penney's people got scared because they knew if they gave those signs and things out, Negroes weren't going to shop there.

Betty Brown

I went on in the store. Why? 'Cause I wanted to. Yeah, because I thought something was in there I wanted, but they was too high, you know, and I didn't have much money, so I just went on out.

— How did you feel about going into the store when the pickets had asked you not to?

Just like I felt before they asked me.

— Have you ever heard the phrase "Black Power"?

Yeah, I've heard of black power. They hold hand up like that and said "Black Power." I seen some men do it around here. And we were doing it in school. I was just doing it because everybody else was doing it. You know, walk down the hall, hold your hand up, say "Black Power." It was something to do.

Have I heard of the riots? Yeah, where they break into the place and burn the place down and steal out of it?

— What do you think about them?

They shouldn't do it. I don't know why, it just isn't right. I don't know why they do it, I guess they just trying to be bad.

•   •   •

— Are you proud or ashamed or neutral about being black?

No, I'm not ashamed of being black. Not at all. Ain't nothing to be ashamed of. I'm proud of it. I know some Negroes that Negroes call white peoples — "There go that white lady right there." You know, because they act strange like they don't wanna be bothered with you and they think they're more than you are. So they call 'em white.

— Do you think that any Negroes ever attempt to hold other Negroes down?

Some Negroes don't want the others to have as much as they got. They sort of act strange. Like, they start acting stubborn, stuck up. Like there are a few Negroes around here that are pretty well off. Most of 'em act like they think they're more than others. Those that got fine houses and pretty fine cars, you know, pass by you with their nose turned up. Just because I had more than peoples I wouldn't act stuck up. I act natural, just like I act now.

And then they some that ain't got much, they still act sort of strange sometime. Like, two people staying side by side, and this person's got electric lights, telephone, a stereo, television, an electric stove and refrigerator. Well, the other person got everything they got except a television. And then they get a television. Then the other person, they'll try to get something else to keep them from having as much as they got.

Like we used to live next door to these people. They had everything we had, and I think we didn't have no stereo. And they had one. So our record player tore up and we got a stereo. And then they got something else that we didn't have, you know. They said they weren't going to let us catch up with them. But we weren't trying to catch up with them. The children just wanted one and Betty got it.

— If you were born again, would you want to be white or Negro?

Negro. I don't know why. I'd just want to be born colored. I guess because I'm colored. And I guess if I was white, I'd rather be born white because I was white.

— Would you rather be born white in a rich family or colored in a poor family?

Colored. Because I'm colored now, I don't wanna be white.

— What are the best and worst things about being a Negro?

I'm gon name the worse thing. You can't get what you want because you don't have enough money to get it. And the best thing, when you do get something, you enjoy it because you don't often get something you really want. Instead of getting everything you want, you know, just getting it, getting it, getting it . . . If you get everything you want, then when you really want something and get it, you don't really enjoy it.

·   ·   ·

— What's the law like around here?

They're bad, by locking peoples up. It's like, if a man be drinking and driving but not drunk, they'll lock him up anyway. And they're bad about getting untax-paid liquor if you have any. My stepfather, he's been locked up. He got locked up one time for shooting a man in the leg, and he got locked up once for fighting and being drunk and driving without a license and selling untax-paid liquor.

— Can you remember some times when people were locked up when they shouldn't have been?

One time a man and his wife, they got to fighting, and the police, they locked up both of 'em, and they shouldn't of locked up nobody but the man because it was him doing it all.

·   ·   ·

What confuses me most about life? You ever heard the statement "The world coming to an end"? That confuses me. I've been wondering when it gon come, how much longer we got. And I be thinking about whether I'll be finished school before the world come to an end or is it coming this year. Will I be done married or have any children?

You know, I read in the Bible that before the world come to an end, it will be a food shortage. You know. A lot of wars, nation against nations, fighting. And, you know those things is happening in the world today. And I be thinking about it.

I think about the saying that everybody got to die. I been wondering when my time coming, when my mama's time coming, you know, how long it gon be? You know, they say you talk back to old people, you showing your days. You know, I'm a little sassy sometime. I get scared. You know, I say something to them before I know it.

•   •   •

— If you could be born as somebody else, who would you like to be?

Jo Ann Parks, a girl at our school. She real pretty, got long hair, fine, got a neat shape, everything. She got a nice personality. And she real light. I told you I think real light folks is cute.

— If you had to be born again, who would you definitely not want to be?

Ida, I don't know her last name. She stay in Daisy. She real dark and she got real long teeth and they sort of hang out of her mouth. She ugly. And real skinny and stuff.

•   •   •

When did I feel the most ashamed of myself? Oh, I got natural-born drunk! And I was with Don, my boyfriend then, and so he used to go with a girl in Williamston named Gloria Ramsey. And so he was taking a boy to Williamston. And he asked the boy did he live over there by Gloria Ramsey, and I slapped him. I knew he used to go with her. And I started mashing the foot speed, the gas, and the car was going real fast, and everybody was hollering to make me stop. And, anyway, he stopped his car and he was gon get me out and talk to me. But I fell in the middle of the highway! And then I went to get back up — he was helping me up — and he asked me could I stand up. And I told him yeah, and when I stood up, I walked over and fell in a ditch, a muddy ditch! Oh, I was *so* embarrassed the next day when they was telling me about it.

•   •   •

My biggest problem growing up has been boys. I don't understand them. I just can't understand them. If you treat them nice, you know, it look like they

don't treat you nice, they don't seem to appreciate it. And if somebody who like you and you don't like them, well, they treat you nice. I don't understand it myself.

. . .

— What would you like to change about yourself?

I would like to turn back the hands of time and start all over again. You done heard that record? I wouldn't do a lot of things that I done did. Like going with a married man. Heap of things. Personal things I don't wanna tell you.

. . .

— What are the three things that are worrying you the most?

Boys, I ain't kidding, they worry me. And my girlfriends, they worry me too. We done had a bad falling out. You see, they jealous, you know, if I be with one more than I be with the other one. They get mad and they'll stop speaking, and that worry me.

And another one, I'm scared I might flunk in math. You see, I don't understand our teacher, I don't understand how he be teaching. You know, he'll be talking this minute and the next minute he be asleep, and you can't understand what he be saying because he talk funny! All the students be talking and you can't hear what he be saying because he don't talk loud.

And then he'll flunk you. One day he gave everyone in the room a book. But he didn't give some of the children a book, like he didn't give me one and Vera and Marilyn. But, anyway, he told everybody to get an assignment out, but I didn't have no book, so we asked him, "Can we go get us a book?" And he said yes. But when all three of us went to walk out, he called us back and we asked could we go get the book. He said, "Don't be hollering at me."

I said, "I wasn't hollering at you, I was just telling you." I guess he thought I got smart with him, but I wasn't meaning to. And he said, "Your attitude ain't too good, is it?" I said, "I'm sorry, I didn't holler." And then I got called to the office.

And then, you know, after the six-week period was up, I had a D in conduct in math class and a C— in grading, and I get my lesson, I don't know how come he gave me that.

One day he called on me for something. And I said, "I didn't come to school yesterday." No, I was at school, I was in the clinic, I didn't go to his room. And he said, "You don't like my class no way." And I said, "Yes, I do." You know, he was talking like that. And I got mad with him, I didn't say nothing, I just started laughing. Started to put me out. Say he gon put me out if I don't shut up. I didn't say nothing. I just turned my head and kept a'smiling; I was so mad . . .

· · ·

— What do you think people who don't know you well think of you?

They probably think I'm pretty nice; then again they might think I'm pretty bad. In the way I act. Like I might turn up my nose or snatch my head or roll my eyes, or not dance when somebody ask me.

· · ·

I ain't scared to fight. If anybody bother me, I don't care how big they is, how little they is, how wide they is, how strong they is, how weak they is, if they bother me and want to fight, *definitely* we'll fight. They'll beat me up too if they can because I be trying to beat them up.

· · ·

— Do you have any objective in life?

Any goals that I want to reach? Finishing school. Boy, I wanna do that badder than anything in the world, I think.

Why? You know, because I'm rather fast, you know. So most people think I ain't gon finish school, but see I want to show everybody that I am. I'm gon finish school, I ain't kidding. You know, even our counselor at school, he called me to his office the other day and had a talk with me. See, he had heard about that fight where I cut Lenora's sleeve with my razor, and he told me that I shouldn't be out fighting, that I was a smart girl, that I shouldn't of been doing that. He said if I had of got locked up, the first thing they would of said, "The captain, the best guard on the basketball team, in jail!" You know, he said that would of been embarrassing to me and it would of been embarrassing to the school too.

But I'm gon show 'em that I'll finish. You know, a heap of peoples, just about everybody — even my kinfolk — don't think I'm gon finish school, you know. Because I sort of go when I wanna, you know, and I can come back when I wanna. You know, they figure that anybody who can go when they wanna and come when they please, I guess they think I'll get pregnant or something. But I ain't though; I ain't kidding, I ain't.

Felton Jones

Felton Jones belongs to a large, close-knit family centered around his stalwart mother. All except one of his brothers and sisters have moved, but they often return to the large but dilapidated house on the outskirts of Adamsville where Felton, his mother, father, brother, and several of his nieces and nephews live. Felton looks older than his age and seems more sturdy and serious-minded than many seventeen-year-olds. The tone of his voice often indicates a genuine and almost childlike curiosity about the world around him.

My first memory is when I got my finger cut. It was almost cut off. We was real small — I was about five — and my brother, my nephew, and me, we was out in the woods cutting wood for the stove. So my nephew and I, we had a little game, you know, who could stick their hand on the chopping block and leave it there the longest, snatch it back before the ax hit down. So that day, I don't know, something happened. I stuck my finger down there and looked off and by that time it got almost cut off. The skin on one side was holding it. Went to the doctor and he sewed it back on.

• • •

I was born August 5, 1952, in Adams County. When we were small, we were staying way out in the country. We never get a chance to come out, you know, like around Adamsville and some place like that. We probably didn't come out of those woods but about once or twice a year. You never had a chance to go nowhere. See, we didn't have no way to go nowhere. Oh, my daddy used to drive this old car but, you know, he drink liquor, so he never did stay around, so we stay there. Unless we take a walk and actually it's too far to walk to Adamsville or something like that.

See, we used to live on the farmland, kind of way out on the back places. A peach orchard, a big peach farm. See, long then, whoever your daddy worked for, you lived in his house. And after you grow up, you go to work for the man yourself.

What do I think of that system? I don't dig it myself. It's all right actually, but the money he pay you to work, it's not enough. When I was eight years old I worked out in the peach orchard then. I worked about a month. All the rest of the peoples was out there picking peaches, and me and my nephew had to be there with the boxes and they'd empty the peaches into the boxes when they get a bagful, and we'd carry peaches for all of 'em. It was hard work and they didn't pay nothing, so my sister — she didn't want us to work no way — told us to quit.

The next time I started working out there, I was about eleven. I worked for a dollar a day, carrying peach boxes. We were working about ten hours a day. A dollar a day. That's right. What I made I'd buy something for next year school, you know, like pants and such a thing. I never had too much money after giving mama part of it. So I worked that time for one year. I quit.

Then Mr. Hudson, the man who own the peach orchard, he told us the next year he would start paying two dollars a day, so I went back to work about three weeks and then I left and went to Atlanta to work. I was about thirteen then and I went to Atlanta and stayed with my brother during the summer. He was a brick mason and I worked as a laborer. Since then, I've worked every summer in Atlanta.

I didn't work on the peach orchard again till this year. Me and my nephew work for him after school. We work only when he needs us, doing all kinds of things. He pays a dollar and thirty cents an hour. It's better than a dollar a day. But it's still not enough. At least, I'd rather have about a dollar and a half an hour, because a dollar and thirty cents, it's actually not enough.

— Why do you think he went up?

Actually, I think he went up because he couldn't get too much help. You know, everybody starting to quit him. So he went up.

— Do you think he could have gone up because he felt the pay wasn't fair?

No, I doubt it that anyone around here would go up for that. They just don't pay you much around here.

When I was getting a dollar a day, my daddy, he was loading the peaches after the boxes had been filled on a big truck that haul 'em to the packing house. He was making, I imagine, round about eight dollars a day. That wasn't nothing. At the time, he had about ten kids in the family to take care of. By the time he got through paying his debts, he still didn't have nothing. Now, he gets a dollar and thirty cents an hour, same as me.

About the only time you can make any money is during peach season. Because if you picking peaches, he pay you by the bag, probably make twelve cents a bag and then you can make eighteen or twenty dollars a day picking. See, some days you make good money, some days you make only two or three dollars. Because if you just going into pick peaches for the first time, the peaches not as ripe as they would be the third time you go in picking. You make some money the third time.

If you make too much money, they get mad and don't want to pay you because they figure you cheat 'em some kind of way. But you can't cheat 'em, because these white ladies that sit up on the wagon there, every time you bring a bucket of peaches there, they give you a ticket. And then in the evening time, they'll count your tickets up and then they pay you off. Like if I was to go out there and make twenty dollars or something like that a day, shoot, they'll start talking — talking about, "I don't believe he picked that many peaches," something like that. That's one reason I quit. Yeah, they'll pay you, but they'll talk about it a long time.

Like if you was to go to another orchard for the first time the peaches just be getting ripe and you make about five or six dollars, then they'll probably say, "What happened to him today, he didn't make that much today." And then after you pick about two or three times and make that much money again, it's the same old thing all the time. Mr. Hudson's wife used to pay off, she'll say, "That boy didn't pick that many peaches," or something like that. If you didn't know no better, they would give you two or three dollars and let you go.

Like one Saturday about two years ago my nephew and I was up there and he had one of these big tractor trailer trucks, and it took us from seven o'clock that morning till one that evening to unload some baskets, some half-bushel baskets. And when they paid us off, you know, I thought maybe they'd give us about ten dollars for unloading. But they gave us two dollars, said they was paying four dollars a day and we didn't work but half a day. You know, I looked at him like that, he looked at me, so I didn't say nothing. I just walked on off.

— What do you do with the money you make now?

See, like each one of us have a different responsibility. I pay some kind of bill, one of 'em pay light bill and something like that. We never keep all of it, we keep part of it, you know, to go to school off of. Get clothes and stuff like that. See, ever since I was young I always give my mama part of the money, so now it just became a part of me. Whatever I make, I give her half of it. I never take it all for myself.

·   ·   ·

My father's sixty, my mother's fifty-nine.

My mother's been pretty tight on me. Yeah, she's pretty strict. She don't let nothing get out of order, she keep everything straight. She used to give me two or three whippings a day. Long in then, it kind of made me mad, but if she hadn't I'd be rough now. I know I would.

Now, she don't want us to get out of place or nothing. If she tell you something, she want you to do it. *Nooo*, I ain't never argued with Mama. She wouldn't stand for that. If I did, I imagine she'd probably get something to hit me with. No, never, I never talked back to Mama.

— Do you ever get mad at her?

Yeah, I get mad. It be real tight not to say nothing. It real bad, but I go out and forget about it. You know, if I go out and sit by myself awhile, I done forgot about it.

My mother, she's the boss of the family. She makes the decisions, then tells my father, then she pass it around. Sometimes he don't agree with it, but it still will go. Whatever she says goes.

— Do you think the man or the woman should run a house, or does it matter?

I think the man should run the house, but in some cases a man . . . For instance, the reason I think my mother run the household is because my daddy used to drink a lot and he never did be home all that much. So that tell her she had to take care of all the responsibilities, so actually she was the head. I think that in most cases around here it's the woman that run the house. As far as I seen, it seems like it's the woman. But I really think it's the man's responsibility.

My mother, I get along better with her than my father. At times, my mother, she like to carry on a whole lot of fun, but my daddy, he don't say nothing too much. You know, he just like to sit around . . . Most of the time he be mad, every time I see him. You know, he don't exactly be mad, he just real mean. He don't want you to sit up too late, you know; I reckon he want us to go to bed like a baby or something, go to bed about eight o'clock. Like after nine

o'clock he don't want you to play the television, nothing like that. See, he be mad because he have to get up early in the morning to go to work, and he think about us being up late, and he can't sleep, or something like that. You know, I like him but I don't like to be around him all that much.

About the maddest I been at my daddy, that's been about four or five years ago. I wanted to go to Atlanta one summer to work, and he want me to go out in the peach orchard with him. So I didn't wanna go. So that Saturday night I called my brother — that's Joe Lee — to come and get me. He came down here to get me.

So when I got ready to go, I told my daddy, I said, "Daddy, I'm fixing to go now." So he told me I wasn't going nowhere. So I actually didn't wanna go out in the peach orchard, because I wasn't making no money out there. So my mama, she told me I could go ahead on. So when she told me I could go, I just went on. My daddy got mad. I was mad too; I didn't wanna stay down here. He told me, "If you go, don't you never come back here no more." So I said, "Well, I'm going then." I just walked on out the house.

I don't know why he wanted me to stay. I reckon he's so crazy about Mr. Hudson out there, the man he work for that own the peach orchard. You know, every year after I quit working out there in the summer, he used to come home and tell me, "I got you a job driving a tractor," or something like that. But I

never did fall for that. See, if you be somewhere driving a tractor, he ain't gon pay you nothing no way. You have a better chance picking peaches; while you picking peaches, you can make fifteen, sixteen dollars a day. But you can't make no money no other time.

The maddest I ever been at my mother? Like, when I used to work in the peach orchard during the summer and you get paid off every other week, and like every Friday she'd buy something new for in the house, and then tell me, "You got to pay for this here." Like this rug right here, and that sofa over there, she bought that. So that take all your money right there and you don't have *nothing* then.

— If you could make one wish for your mother and father that would come true, what would it be?

I would wish that they could get a home of their own because my mother, she been wanting a home a long time. So I wish one day she can get it.

•   •   •

There are twelve of us brothers and sisters in all living. I had one brother who died when he was a baby. He died before I was born. I think that he had pneumonia, died when he was born. He was born at home, not in a hospital. My mother brought all her children into the world at home, never went to a hospital. Not but two home now, me and my younger brother.

These others that live here, those are my little nieces and nephews. Five of 'em. The two little boys, one of 'em is my brother's and the other's my sister's. They both live in Atlanta. The kids, they'd rather live down here than live up there. Actually, they rather for 'em to live down here 'cause in Atlanta they'll be in the street and they're scared something will happen to 'em, they might get run over playing in the street. And the three girls don't want to go to school in Atlanta.

Joe Lee, he's my favorite brother. Lives in Atlanta. He give me most anything I want. Like if I need money or something, he give it to me. Most of 'em just say they ain't got it. But if Joe Lee got any, I get it from him. I remember the sweetheart ball this year, I didn't need no money but I needed a car. See, we don't have no car here. So he didn't have one himself at the time but he told me he'd borrow one and he did and he lent it to me. When I need a car to go out somewhere I mostly borrow Joe Lee's car. If I call him and tell him that morning, he'll probably bring it to me that evening. He say he know how it is because when he was coming up he didn't have no way around. So he doesn't want me to be like that.

Now, my oldest brother, Walter Jr., he kind of wanna be a big shot, something like that. The whole family get together about once a month, we have a party, have a good time. And he, you know, he got a lot of money and when everybody get together, he got two or three thousand dollars in his pocket and he be flashing his money, going on. So everybody get mad with him. As soon as he get in a crowd, he be flashing his money. You know, he don't have to worry about nothing, got a pocketful of money and a brand new car.

•   •   •

Yeah, I consider my family poor. Yeah, we have to be. You know, we have clothes and things but not what we want, you know, far as a home or something like that. I consider ourself poor. Don't have no money, nothing. Just got some clothes, that's all. This old furniture, it ain't nothing. Reason we ain't got any, this house, it ain't appropriate for any furniture or nothing. You know, it rains in this place. It rains and starts dropping through here any minute. I don't like it. It just rain in it and the rooms are so big you can't get 'em warm. It be real cold in the winter. See, actually it's real hard work in the winter because you have to get wood and burn it through your fireplace; it take a lot of wood. And we probably get a big truckload every other week, take a lot of wood, a lot of work. And a lot of flies get in here in the summertime. They come through anywhere, windows and things.

Now, this man my daddy and me work for who own this house, he used to try to keep it up, but he says he ain't gon repair it no more, says he was losing out on it or something or nuther.

— How do you feel about that?

I believe he got what he want, his home all right. If we want to stay here, we repair it ourselves — I imagine that's the way he feel about it. I don't feel bad about it all because, you know, it's his house . . . In a way I think we should repair it; you know, we could put a window or something in, but as far as fixing the top, I don't think we should do that. If he would sell it to us, we probably do it. But it's not our house, it's his responsibility to fix it. And at least, my daddy, he don't pay too much rent, but the little he pay — about ten or fifteen dollars a month — the little he pay, he should.

Now, we've been trying to build a house for five years. We've been trying to build one of our own. We've been trying to buy some land at the fork of the road there, but the lady, she wouldn't sell it. And we tried to buy a house down the road here. We didn't have the cash money, so we intended to finance it, and something happened. The loan wouldn't finance that kind of house. But I think

by next year, we'll be able to build a house. After we get the land, my brother would build it, see. He's a brick mason. If we could get the land, see, one of my brothers said he would buy all the blocks and things that it took, and one of 'em, he said he would build it, and the rest of 'em said they'd chip in and get everything else it needs.

My mama is the main one that wants another house. She says she wants to get out of this house. See, for instance, when it rains there're a bunch of leaks. When it rains, she get up and she be fussing and telling about she going to get out of this old shack before it fall down on her.

— Could you describe the differences between the houses of black people and white people?

I'm Somebody Important 54

Most Negroes, you can tell their house anywhere. Because they ain't got nothing but a raggedy old shack, you know, old wood and stuff falling off it. And all white peoples, they got big fine brick homes. All those chandelier lights in the houses — you know, you ride by in the road and see in the windows they got little candles and things with lights on it. You can tell the white peoples' houses from the Negroes'. Negroes — I can't say all Negroes because some Negroes in Adams County got nice houses — but most Negroes have houses like this one, just an old raggedy wood house, about to fall down on them.

— What do you think about that?

Well, the white, they have to have something or nuther nice because they get the Negroes to work for 'em. They won't pay 'em nothing, so they making all the money and everything. They got all the money, they got to have something.

— Where do you get your water?

We got a well out here. We have a bucket, haul the water in it.

— How do you feel about that?

I don't like it. Every time we get ready for some water, we have to run way out there and draw up a bucketful, while if we had running water, just turn it on and get the water. I reckon one day, in the near future, we might be able to get running water. For the time being, it's all right. If it was our own house, we *would* have running water, but since this is Mr. Hudson's house . . . See, if we have running water put in here, he probably put us out as soon as my daddy's disabled to work or something like that.

We have an outside toilet, an outhouse. I don't like to use it. Everybody using it, you know, and you can't flush it down, just all the waste and all this stuff be in it, just right down there. I just don't like them. Not at all. Most of the time, you know, I don't never use the toilet at home. Most of the time I be at school, use it at school. Sometimes, like on the weekends, probably use here.

— Do you always have enough food?

No. See, when we was young, we used to plant peas, sweet potatoes, most everything you raise on a farm. We had a little patch. But now we don't have no farming so each month the government give us this surplus food. You get some of that. But I don't like that food. It don't taste right, it got a different taste. They give you some peas you can't cook; you can cook 'em all day and they still be hard-like. It ain't good to me. They used to give us this prune juice, but they stopped giving it because it wasn't nobody drink that stuff. I don't care too much about that food.

— Do you ever think of reasons for your being poor?

Felton Jones   55

No, I haven't really sat down and thought about it. One day I hope to have something. You know, I know I'm not never gon get what I really want, but I have more than I have now.

— Do you think there's any possibility that you might be poor when you are grown?

No, I'd say about five more years from now, I'll be doing all right for myself.

— Do you think anyone powerful cares about poor people?

No, not around Adamsville. I don't guess whites care too much. But you know, as much as the Negro has to do, they get out there, some of 'em go out here and raise the peach crop for the white man, and then some of 'em, they work in the white folks' houses, and then after the white man gets what he wants, he don't care nothing about 'em then. He don't care what happens to 'em after that.

•　　•　　•

— What's important to you?

Now, mostly only thing that's real important is my education. Real important. I want to get one.

— Why?

To get a good job, I believe. You know, I don't wanna be out there slaving no harder than I already doing.

— Do you think you'll finish school?

Uh-huh, I *know* I am! One time I thought about dropping out. I couldn't do it though. It was about two years ago I started to drop out. I just got tired of going so I decided I was gon quit. I went to Atlanta on a Sunday night and stayed there Monday at my brother's, this was Joe Lee. But he told me, "Don't drop out, got to go on back." And he gave me bus fare, so I came on back. That's what changed my mind — he asked me, "What you going to do after you quit?" I told him, "I go to work." He said, "Work where?" I said, "I don't know." So I came on and went back to school.

— Did Joe Lee finish school?

No, Joe Lee, he didn't go to school too much at all. I had four sisters and a brother to finish school — Raymond. And I had one brother that quit in about the second semester of the twelfth grade. One day he left and went to school, came back home and walked away, don't never know what happened; he been gone ever since.

I really like school. It's something that just become a part of me, I don't know why. It's fun in some classes, it don't be boring all the time. Like if you

have a good teacher. A good teacher is when you go to her class, you have something exciting every once in a while. You don't just sit in the classroom and just down in a book all the while you're in there. It's not interesting that way. But if you're in there and go to the book and look at something and then come back and just discuss the whole thing, you know, without the book, and then she probably say something to keep the class alive . . .

Have I ever been whipped in school? Oh, yeah, all until I was in the sixth grade. Some had leather straps and some used a switch, and in high school now they have a little board about four inches wide and eighteen inches long. All the teachers have a different paddle. All the boys that take shop, they probably got to make one apiece to give to teachers. It's about an inch thick, have it trimmed at the end so they can get a good grip on the handle so they can whip you with it better. I'd let 'em whip me now but not with that. Not with a board. Now, a bunch of the students, they get hit with it, but I don't go for it. Most all the teachers do it in high school. All of 'em use the board except for ones in homemaking.

They mostly hit you for not doing your lessons. But I don't think it's right for 'em to whip you 'cause of that. See, they could punish you another way. But if they whip you because of homework, next time they tell you to bring something in, you ain't gon try to get it right, you just throw something together and take it on. Just so you have it. In high school, I don't think they should have it, because after you get in high school you supposed to be old enough, mature enough, to know right from wrong. I don't know if they hit you in the white school. I don't think so though.

I was going to go over to the white school for this year. You know, we have a choice form to fill out. Actually, I didn't fill mine out; my sister filled it out. See, when my form came in the mail, I was in Atlanta, so my sister filled it out. So she filled it out for Carver, the Negro school. I *was* planning on going to the white school. It's a lot of colored students over there. You know, it's not that many but it's a right smart of 'em.

I believe they have better classes over there than we do. You know, the way teachers is, from the white teachers I've been around, I'd like to go over there. Until we got this white teacher over at our school, I hadn't been around white peoples that much to know what they were like.

And I'd have better equipment too. Because actually we don't have *nothing*. They have music, guitars, they teach you how to play guitars over there and everything. But at our school, a chorus is the only thing they got. We don't even have a band.

Now, the main reason I'd wanna go over there is this: The only way if you wanna learn something at Carver, you gon have to go ahead and do it on your own, because most of the kids, they're just there to be there. At our school, all through the day about twenty or thirty or fifty students in the hall, all day long, just clowning and going on. I don't believe it's like that at the white school. They don't allow it out there. But you can't learn nothing at Carver. Actually, a place like that might as well turn into a nightclub or something like that. You know, they do some of everything there. You see groups sitting around, some of 'em gambling, some of 'em drinking beer and liquor and stuff. And then some of 'em smoking dope, smoking aspirin and BC powder, you know, getting out of their head and talking a whole lot of trash and cutting fool and going on.

— Do you study much?

Yeah, I study a lot, have to. Every night I study; I have to try to get out of school. I got 'bout a C+ average now and I'm in the eleventh grade. I thought one time I'd be glad to get out, I been thinking about that, but I see the responsibility after you get out of school — you have to go work, you on your own then.

• • •

Actually, when I finish high school, I'm gon go to trade school and take up a trade and from there I'm going into the Navy. They have it now that after you finish the eleventh grade, instead of going to the twelfth grade, you go to trade school. I'll probably go to trade school for two years. I can go one year free in Thomaston, and the next year I'll have to pay for it myself so I'll go to Atlanta. I had in mind to take up business administration, IBM. See, when I was young, my brother had a little typewriter, he could type real good. And I used to tell him, "One day I'm gon be better than you is." So I got in the ninth grade, I took up general business and business math so I could take typing the next year, and so I been taking typing ever since. I think I can get him now. See, IBM about the same as typing, you got pretty much the same keyboard.

My mama, she wanted me to go to college. But I don't know. I used to want to go, but I don't wanna go now. I don't know why Mama wants me to go. You know, my brother who finished school, he said he was going to college, but he didn't go. I had a sister, she said she was going, so after she finish school she went to Atlanta to work. Mama wants one out of twelve to go. She says one out of twelve ought to do something. I still might end up going, but it might fall on my younger brother. He probably will go. If I really wanted to, I could do it, if I really wanted to. But I ain't never thought too much about going to college.

Actually, after I finish school I was intending to go into the Navy. Spend ten, fifteen, or twenty years, then I'll retire. See, actually, I saw this man, he was in the Navy and came to the school year before last, and he had on these stripes. You know, he was real pretty where he had all those stripes on his arm. And I said then if I ever get old enough to go into the Navy, I'm going. Because I know if I could get those — he had those stripes all up and down his sleeve, a new uniform, you know, real neat.

I'll spend about ten or fifteen years in the Navy and then I'll retire. After I retire, I'll come back — right back here to Adams County — build me a home and settle down. See, after you retire, the Navy support you; I think they'll give me enough money to support myself.

— Do you believe there are people who don't want to see you make good?

Yeah, it's some. I have some classmates, some of 'em don't want to see you make it. But I don't believe nothing can stop me now. It's too far gone. But, you know, some of my classmates, we came up from elementary school together, and we was doing all right. So, lately, after we got to Carver, and they met new friends up there, then they start flunking out. And once they start flunking, they try to encourage you not to go to class or something like that. But, no, I can't cut no classes. It's too far gone.

— What would you think if you ended up with the same job as your father?

I don't know what I'd do then, if it ended up like that. If it ended up like that, I think I'd be crazy myself. At least, I'd try to get out of it. I just probably wouldn't do nothing if I had to do that. I'd hang around the corner rather than do that; just hang around the corner.

•　　•　　•

— When was the happiest time of your life?

When was the happiest time of my life? It was when I had this birthday party, it was a surprise birthday party my sister gave me. She invited all my girl-friends and all of 'em was here. It was, you know, real exciting. Because actually I didn't even know nothing about it until I got here.

•　　•　　•

The most terrifying thing I ever seen happen . . . It was when I saw this man kill this man about a cigarette. It was a bunch of boys, we was standing on the street in Atlanta. So they was these mens up there, you know, they was having a good time, so this man snatched a cigarette out of this man's hand. So the man that got his cigarette snatched away, he didn't say nothing, he just kept walking around there. And then before we even knew it — we was standing right there — he just pulled his gun out of his pocket and just started shooting. He shot the man through the head about three times. After he shot him, he didn't even run or nothing, he just stood there, just looked at him. So when the man fell on the street, blood just ran down the street.

And then last summer in Atlanta, I saw two men on the street corner, they joined hands — each one had a knife in his hand — and they was cutting each other. Each time one cut the other one, the other one cut him. You know, "I cut you, you cut me, I cut you, you cut me." Just cut different parts of the body. They died just laying down, cut each other to death. Actually they were just cutting and laughing, they just kept cutting and laughing.

•   •   •

I was eight years old when I joined the church. The night I joined, Thursday night, my sister and I were sitting in the church, and so the preacher said, "All sinners come to the front." I didn't know what he said and my sister told me to get up and go to the front. Actually, he forced me to do it. Because I didn't know what was going on. He came around, he shook my hand, asked me did I want to join the church. I said no, not right then. He said, "Don't you remember this is a Baptist church? If you want to be a child of God, you have to join the church." So I told him, yeah, I'll join the church, like that.

•   •   •

I read the paper quite often. The *Atlanta Constitution*. I always read the front page. See, actually, I don't get a chance to see it until I get to school because we don't get it at home. First thing when I get to school in the morning I get the paper and read it. We have about twenty minutes before we get to class so I go to the library and sit there and read it.

•   •   •

The worst thing about Adamsville? It have to be the working conditions around here. You know, there no jobs or *nothing* here. It's all right living here but you just can't make no money here. You have to go someplace else to make the money and then come back. Like I don't think Joe Lee — you know, my brother — like Atlanta too good, because he always be down here. If he didn't have to work, he be down here tonight; most of the time he be down here through the week. I think he lives there because he can make more money up there than he can in a rural area. In Adams County, actually, there's nothing for you to do but go to work on a farm, something like that. 'Less you get a job in Columbus and that's over thirty-five miles.

I wouldn't wanna live in Atlanta, but I rather work there. But I don't wanna live there. I don't like up there. It's all right to work there, but the surrounding, I don't like it. The people, at least in the neighborhood where I was staying at, they was drinking, going on, carrying on all the time, be fighting and going on. I never liked that. Down here you might find somebody get drunk but they probably go home after. But up there, see, get in the street, they do anything.

So far I like the country better. Because city life . . . See, the air and stuff, it's too close up there. You need to get out in the open so you can get some fresh air; there's no fresh air up there. All that stuff, factories and stuff there. I like the country better. See, you can do most anything in the country. In the city you have to kind of be particular what you do because if you get wrong, they probably lock you up up there. In the city you have to be careful what you do. It's too close up there.

· · ·

— Did your parents ever tell you anything about race when you were a young child?

No. Well, my mama always tell me to go to school and get a good education, because one day you gon need it. She used to say, "Try to do something for yourself because the white man, all he after is to get you out there to work for them and they making the money." She been telling me this for a long time, ever since I been big enough to know. You know, at first, I never did think much about what she said too much, but now I really see she was right.

What will I tell my own kids? Probably tell them like my brother tells me. He say, "Felton, you growing up now, you big enough to go on your own. You can't go out there and be no white man's fool." Says, "If you gon be a fool, be a Negro's fool." And say, "Every penny you get, don't just take it to the white man, save it or put it to some good use." Joe Lee tells me this. Reason he tell me all this, I reckon he gon try to get something out of me one day.

— When did you first learn about being a Negro and all that means?

Well, it's been about five or six years ago that I first learned about being a Negro. There wasn't any particular instance that made me realize it, I just gradually realized it. You know, I always heard them talking about it but I never did get a chance to be around white people too much until I got big enough to work a little. So after then I saw how the white man was, and how he do to the Negro, have them out there working for nothing. Because I know my mama says a long time ago they used to work for a quarter or something like that for a day. I know I worked for a dollar. I thought that was real bad but she said they worked for less than that.

— How did you feel when you realized this?

It didn't take too much effect on me then, because, you know, that's about the only choice I had then. You know, I just had to get out there and work. But now, it's different now.

You know, what I was trying to do was get a better understanding of all of it, just work my way up to it, get a picture of it. Then after I understood what was going on, I would try to let 'em know that I was the same as they was. Ever since I got up in some size they be talking, you know, "Hey, boy." I say "Yeah, what you want?," something like that. Then they want you to say *sir* to 'em. But I just talk to 'em. If they say "Boy," I say, "Huh?" They wanted you to say *sir* but I never did dig it.

This here David — he's Mr. Hudson's son, Mr. Hudson own this here peach orchard — when he was about seven years old he wanted you to say "Mister David," something like that. Then I was about thirteen. Actually, he'll just tell you, say, "I don't want you to call me David, I want you to say *mister*," something like that. It never did change, I kept calling him David.

Most all the whites I been around, they always call a Negro by his first name. I don't think it's right for 'em to do that. Actually I don't. I know my daddy, I think he was sixty in January. And, see, this man he works for, he has another son, named Roy, he's not but about thirty-five years old, and every day, "Walter, get the truck, and meet me out here in the morning." Then, if my daddy asks something: "Mr. Roy, you want me to come over in the truck this morning?" something like that. Actually, it's not right for him to do it. But I think if he was to stop saying *mister* to him, you know, until he recognize him as an older person, I think that they will change a little. You know, like if they want to be recognized themself as *mister*, they'll have to call him *mister*.

Actually, that's what I've been trying to get my daddy to see. Like my daddy says, "Mr. Roy, I want to borrow your truck to go somewhere," or like that. I told him, I said, "Daddy, you have a kid older than Roy is." I said, "You don't have to worry about calling him Mr. Roy, like that." But he don't like nobody to tell him something like that. He gets mad — you know, talking about, "You do it your way, I'll do it my way."

And he's like this. Like on Sunday, if Mr. Hudson want him to do something and he fixing to go to church and like that, he'll just forget about church and do it. Something like that. My mama, she says, "Walter, you ain't nothing but a fool." I don't know what's wrong with him, he still act the same way.

My daddy, he more like a houseboy. You know, when a Negro is crazy about a white man, when he'll do anything for a white man for nothing, call him a houseboy. You know, he'll never change. He like to work for nothing, you know. And actually, he one of those kinds, he kind of scared of the white man.

— Are most Negroes around here afraid of white people?

Some of 'em. Some of 'em not. Ones that are, I don't know why they're scared of 'em. But this man — he used to work out in the peach orchard when I was working out there — and Mr. Hudson come out there to say something and he just jump and go to running. Like if he see him coming, and he be sitting down, he just jump up and go to running. And one day, we were sitting out there eating lunch, and some fellow gave him some cake, and as soon as he got the cake and saw the man coming, he just threw the cake down and jumped up and started back to work and everybody else sitting there eating. He was scared of him.

And some of 'em act stupid, kind of like clowns, around white people. I have a brother-in-law about like that. You know, when he get around whites, he change a lot. Like if a white man was come around and be talking to him, he acts like, you know, "Yes sir, captain, yes sir," you know, a whole lot of jive. And when the white man leaves, he be right back normal.

The way I feel about that, if a person gets right around a man and act like they scared of him, you know, "Yes sir, captain" and all like that — give a white man that compliment — ain't really doing nothing but making him think he got a whole lot of power over him or something like that. And, see, I imagine one reason they want the Negro to call them *mister,* I reckon it make them feel big. Like they are around another white person, this Negro comes up and says "Mr. Roy" or something like that, I believe it make them feel like they a king or something.

— Do you think black women or black men are more afraid of white people?

Men. Some women is like that, but most of 'em not. The reason I say that is that mens is out working every day for the white man and then their wives, they're at home. See, they don't know what's going on. Like the man, he be out there, and like the bossman will tell him to do something, he'll just jump up and run, you know, try to do it before he say anything. Actually, I don't believe a lady would be like that. She might for a while, but actually she'll soon break it. Because I know when I was just working in the peach orchard regular I noticed that then. If a man was out there and they told him to do something, he would jump up and run. But if it was a lady and they told her to do something, she'd do it if she wanted, and then if she didn't wanna, she didn't do it. I don't know why that is. I don't know whether the womens is braver than the mens or what.

•   •   •

— How do you feel toward white people?

It's the same way with whites as it is with Negroes, because it's some bad whites and some bad Negroes, you know. I never am around white people much unless I'm down at the peach orchard working and the bossman come out.

— Do you see any difference between whites and Negroes?

Uh, one difference — the white, they don't like to never associate with a Negro. You know, wherever a Negro, the white man don't like to be around him. But, actually, Negroes, they don't have no other choice but to be around whites. You know, if the white man don't wanna be around them, they can figure out some kind of way to keep from being around 'em.

No, it don't bother me whether I'm around 'em or not. No, it don't matter. In a way I like to be around 'em. Some of 'em is real friendly; some of 'em, they don't care too much about you.

Like this man over here, Edward White, his son. One day I went down there to hunt, so when I was ready to come home, I didn't want to have to go way over to the highway, so I came across his pasture down there. And he raised all kind of sand, you know, like he wanted to whip me or something. He saw me coming across his pasture, he said, "Hey, old nigger, what the hell you doing down there?" So I just walked on across it and he come down there, and I told him I was hunting down there and when I got ready to come home I just came across to come home.

He told me to get my damn ass off his place, told me to never be coming through there or he'll whip the hell out of me or something like that. So I said, "Yeah, man, I was just coming across, so I'm going on." He kept talking and I had a gun with me. He said get off his place 'fore he whipped hell out of me. I know he wouldn't of whipped me because I had a gun in my hand. I didn't say nothing because I was standing right there on his place. I did respect that, but he kept talking and I opened the gun and put a shell in it because I thought maybe he was gon try to whip me sure 'nuf. He kept walking and then he finally stopped about as far from here to that table over there. Then he started again so I thought about it, he might try it sure 'nuf. I would of shot him if he had came any closer.

Me and him was down there in the pasture by ourself and at the time I started to grab him and just whip him pretty good and leave him down there. And then, naw, go on across. So I just went on, like wasn't no trouble. Now, sometimes, his cows get out and come all up here. And he got to come up here to get 'em up, see. He come right through our driveway to see about those cows.

And another white man, yeah, I know this man up here what runs this filling station. Now, I have a little nephew, he's thirteen years old, he can't walk, he can't talk, you know, he ain't got no use for hisself. So one Sunday my sister that live in Crossroads City and I, we had him in a wheelchair and we was rolling him around town. And we stopped by this Shorty's filling station and she went in there to get my nephew a drink. And while he sitting there, he couldn't talk, you know, so he started urinating in the street. My sister had come out and she had gotten about four drinks and some potato chips — she'd gotten about a dollar and a half's worth. And so this white man run out there and he said, "Who that got that nigger out there wetting all over the place?" So my sister, she got mad, just throw the drinks and things down. Then he tried to make her pick 'em up, so they exchanged a few words. He told her to come back and pick up them drinks and she told him she wasn't gon pick up a *damn* thing, said if he wanted to pick 'em up, he could pick 'em up his *damn* self! And he told her he wasn't gon pick 'em up, said if she stay there any longer he'd put the damn man on her. She told him to call the man, it didn't make any difference.

— Tell me about some other examples of prejudice.

You find most white people, they don't want a Negro to come to their house, you know, unless if he come around to the back. They want you to come to the back door and knock. And, you know, if they come to your house, they probably walk around to the front. They won't come in the back door.

Actually, that's the reason I don't go to too many white people's houses, because they want you to come to the back. You know, I have went to white people's houses and they said go around to the back. My nephew and I, we was going to this man's house to sell some pecans. And when we got there, he told us to come on around to the back. So I just turned around and went on back home. My nephew, he went on around to the back and sold the pecans, but I turned around and went back.

— You said you knew some friendly white people.

Like this man, he work in the peach orchard, Mr. Simon Shepherd. You know, he real friendly; he like to have a lot of fun. And when I was working in Atlanta, my brother was the foreman of the concrete, and there was this other man — his name was Joe — he was foreman to construction, and then they had this superintendent. You know, it was two white and then my brother was colored. On Friday, all of 'em go to the store and get a whole lot of beer, come down here to drink it, be around here, having a good time. Then I was friends with these two white boys I was finishing concrete with.

Yeah, there are some white peoples that look at Negroes as equal human beings. Like this insurance lady, well, she real friendly. She try to help the Negro

all she can. Like my sister's little boy was ill, she got the little boy where he can go to school now. She the main cause of it, because my sister, she'd been trying to get him in the hospital a long time, but her by herself, she couldn't get him in. So this here insurance lady, she used to come around once every other week, she'd stop by and stay awhile, and she got him in the hospital.

— What white person you know do you respect the most?

It'd have to be my teacher, Mr. East. You know, because that's about the only white man I be around every day.

• • •

I'm Somebody Important

I think most whites think they're better than Negroes. That's because most whites, they got a lot of money and they got what they want, and most of the Negroes got to get what they want. You know, they already got theirs. Another reason is when a white person get a Negro to say *yes sir* and recognize him *mister*, like that, they think they're really on top.

— How do you feel about most whites having money and most Negroes not having much?

Way I feel about it is this: You know, the white man, he got a lot of money and it's right for him to have it, because the Negro, they could have it. But most Negroes, they get money and then, see, a lot of 'em just drinking and just blow it. And then a lot of 'em go out there and work for nothing. See, if most of 'em was to stop working for nothing, I believe in order for the white man to get anybody to work for 'em they have to pay some money. Because around here, actually, they don't pay nothing.

— What do you think about whites who want to hold Negroes down?

I don't know. But they should try to help 'em because it some real poor Negroes and it some real poor whites, and that way, if they was to help one another along . . . You know, I think if the white and the Negro was to just go on and just get together, the world, it would just be a better place to live. Because you find some Negroes that don't like the whites and you find some whites that don't like the Negro, something like that. There always gon be a big argument, all the time. Never will get nowhere.

But I don't think they ever will get together. Because I know next year at Carver, they supposed to send half of the Negroes to Adams County over there and then half of the whites over here. But I know they gon have a private school, they gon take the Negro school in Pineville and have it for a private school for white. You know, by them doing that, the government, they no longer have any power over the school, because they have to pay to go to school there. And there're some poor white, and there are some whites that ain't gon be able to pay that money to go to school. Some poor whites just like they is colored.

— What do you think of poor whites?

I believe one day in the near future they'll be real wealthy theirself because if they can just stay in school long enough to get their education, they're coming to the top.

— Is the same true with Negroes?

Yeah, with some of 'em, Negroes will too. But not all. Because some Negroes, see, they scared, most of 'em is scared. See, get around a white person, just trembling and going on.

— What changes would you like to see in the majority of whites?

I would just like to see all the Negroes and whites get together and, you know, be friends. Like they ought to get tired of fighting and running all the time, you know. Keeping from being around Negroes. They got these private schools to keep the Negroes from 'em, but sooner or later the Negroes gon be in those private schools with 'em. And I think we ought to just face the problem.

— Are there many black and white friends in Adamsville?

No. Because mostly you hear some say they don't like the whites, and then some say they like the whites, but I don't think it's too many white friends. There're not that many Negroes with a white friend unless they work around each other. But as far as just meeting up and talking, most of 'em say they hate 'em, but I don't know. Some of 'em say they don't want to be around 'em or something like that. But I don't see no difference in it. You know, I just had a lot of experience during the summer in Atlanta and then going to school and having a white teacher. I don't know, it's the same to me.

But most of 'em say the white man, all they want is your money. Say once they get your money, get you out there working for 'em, they through with you. I heard some of 'em say like if you working on the white man's job, he want you to slave, to work for nothing, then after you get off, he forget about you. But actually the way I see it, the white man, he can't make you work for him, you work on your own. The way I feel about it.

But a lot of white people are just like they say. I know the man my daddy works for, he about just like that. You know, once you get sick where you can't work or something like that, he forget about you then. Really you just down. When you get sick you don't have no money, and he don't pay you nothing till you start back work. My daddy got sick and had to stop work around Christmas, he just did go back — and this is April — and he didn't pay him nothing. But my sister and brother in Atlanta, they kept everything going till he started back to work.

See, all of 'em around here, all the whites, they try to get you for as little as they can. The way I feel, it's not right, because once you get out there and work for about forty or fifty dollars a week you don't have — especially a person with responsibility — he don't have no money to do nothing with because prices keep going up. And once he pay rent or something like that, phone bill, buy groceries, he don't have nothing!

— What changes would you like to see in relations between blacks and whites?

One thing, I'd like the black and the white be treated the same. Now mostly the white have an advantage over the Negro. Now, most whites, they go after a job, they can get most any job they want, while a Negro, he probably be there for a while, you know, taking tests and all that old crap. And then a white man, he just walk in there and fill out an application and he's hired.

— Which is more important, integration or equal job opportunities?

Integration would be most important. First, before we can work with anyone we have to first get to know 'em. You can't work with nobody and an enemy at the same time. First, you have to know 'em and make friends.

And, you know, most jobs now they have white employees. Okay, you probably find some whites that can do a job better than a Negro, and then sometimes you find a Negro can do a job better than a white, so if you mix it up, you can see what is what. You know, it won't be no big argument about it, about who gets the job.

•   •   •

— Do you think there's any difference between blacks and whites?

The white, really, they care. But the Negro, they don't care, most of 'em don't care. I can't say it for all of 'em, but most of 'em, they don't care. And you probably hear 'em say, "I don't care." They don't care for nothing, most of 'em. You know, if someone was to come over and say, "John, y'all go vote and make sure that we get a Negro in the chair this year," he'll say, "I don't care if he don't get in," something like that.

— Would you rather work for a white or black?

I'd rather work for a white, for a white. All depends on what the price they paying, but see, when you working for a colored person, most of the time he'll try to cheat you. You know, like he'll tell you he gon pay you something and then when Friday come, time to pay off, he done changed it. Because I know I used to work for a preacher, and he told me he was gon pay two dollars an hour. I worked about forty-eight hours that week and when we got ready to get paid off, he gave me sixty-something dollars. I told him to check if that's right, and he told me yeah, it's right. Said, "See, I ain't paying but a dollar and a half now."

— If you could be born again, would you rather be white or Negro?

Negro. The life I'm living now, it's not excellent, but it's pretty good. Actually, I'd just want to be born Negro. I don't know why.

•   •   •

— What if you suddenly found yourself in the environment of an average well-to-do white?

Felton Jones   73

At first, I'd probably sit around and think about it before I say anything. And then after I see I'm there in the middle of nothing but well-to-do white men, then I'd just . . . you know, control myself. I wouldn't be nervous or scared or nothing like that. I'd get around there and, you know, probably talk to some of 'em and ask questions. And, you know, probably some of 'em make friends but some of 'em, they don't want to be bothered with you.

•　　　•　　　•

— How did you become interested in the racial issues?

Actually, it just became a part of me; you know, every time I hear something about racial, I try to listen and learn something about it, because actually I don't know too much about it. But when I hear something about it I stop and listen, try to find out something. Actually, when you go to school in your history class, you always hear where the white man fought in the war, but you never hear where the black man fought unless he was a slave. So by that, when someone started talking about racial and all that, I just started listening and see how is the black man coming along now. And I see a lot on television and then I read about it. When they turned those school buses over in South Carolina and burn 'em, I saw that and then I got the paper and read it in the paper.

— What would you have done if you were on that bus?

What would I have done? Well, if I was in one and they overturned it, I don't know, I don't know what kind of advance they would have over me. You know, most Negroes, they're scared, most of 'em. If I was sitting up there and had someone to go along with me, we'd probably get back even with them. I'd have to have someone stick with me because I know that me by myself, I couldn't do nothing. The same as they overturned the school bus that we was sitting on, we'd probably wait until they get on a bus and overturn it.

And then I saw another thing on the news where they closed those schools down and they wasn't intending to open 'em back up until they got rid of the Negro. And they sort of hated to go to school with Negroes, so most of 'em went to private schools, but some of 'em still went to the integrated school. Well, see, I don't have no objections to integrated schools. All I want to see is that they get the schools in Adams County integrated. Really, I think it's gon be kind of hard for 'em in Adams County. Because it's a lot of white people that don't want their white kids with Negroes. And I read in the paper the other week where they was buying Pineville School and they gon use it for a private school and there were no Negroes allowed.

— How do you feel when you see on the news some sort of protest by black people?

Actually, what I see on television, I sit and listen real careful, and then it's what they're protesting for, and if it makes sense, it make you feel kind of strong. But then if they're just out there protesting for what don't make sense, actually, it don't make too much difference with me, but most of the time it make sense what they be doing.

The most interesting news event to me was when Dr. Martin Luther King was assassinated. I felt pretty bad. Because at the time I was sitting right there in the hall watching television, and the television went off and they had a special report come on, and they said he had got shot. So I sit there and look almost all night. I sit there about six hours. Every once in a while they had a special report come on and tell you what was happening, and I sit there and watched it until the television went off. And then the next morning I got up real soon and they said what time he died and all. I felt real sad.

— What contributions do you know of that blacks have made to the world?

I'm thinking about Ralph Abernathy. He's about the best one out there. You know, mainly what he's trying to do is carry out what Martin Luther King has already started. But, you know, most people say he's taking the place of King, but the way I see it he can't take the place of King, he have to carry out his work.

And have you ever heard tell of Stokely Carmichael? I saw him, he was talking once in Atlanta. You know, it was a bunch of us standing out in the street, he was coming up the street. He told all of us to come down to the union office Monday morning and if we would join the union that he would get us a job, you know, the brick masons and all the laborers. He said the laborers would make not under three and a half dollars and the brick masons not under five. But didn't nobody go. You know, he carried on a whole lot of fun. You know, we thought he was just jiving around.

— Do you know of any famous Negroes in history?

Oh yeah, George Washington Carver. Booker T. Washington. But actually, see, they don't teach much of that where I go to school. They ought to teach more of it, because most Negroes, they don't even know what's going on. They don't even know who is who, they just here. Because actually, most of 'em, they not gon read that much and only time they gon learn it is to hear somebody talk about it. And it be real interesting discussing the Negro in class. We talk about, you know, about how in the history books you never hear of a colored person, you never see a picture of them or something like that unless it was a slave. So you never hear of a Negro in history. But I think everyone should know something about Negroes, something they did, besides just work on a farm. All you read about is the white man; a Negro never did anything.

So we had a student teacher in American history about a month ago, and he like to refer to the book. And so everybody told him they didn't want to go just right out of the book. And then he said, "Why not?" And then some girl asked, "Why is it that they never have nothing about a colored person and the white man always do everything? The Negro helped fight in the war and different things."

Last year in Negro History Week, everybody had to do a report on a famous Negro. That's about the only time they talk about Negroes in history mostly. This year during Negro History Week, Mr. East, the white teacher, asked the question: "Why do we have Negro History Week? There are fifty-two weeks in the year, who are the other weeks for?" Somebody said, "For the white man." So he said, "You don't think the Negro should have other weeks besides just Negro History Week?" So we had a pretty good discussion on that. I think there should be more during the year, because all the rest is white history weeks — that what Mr. East said.

•   •   •

— Would you be interested in joining some kind of civil rights organization?

Uh, I don't know, I don't know. Something like that you have to think about after it come to you.

— Would you like SCLC, the organization that Dr. Martin Luther King headed, to establish an office in Adamsville?

Yeah. It seems in Adamsville, the whites, actually they don't hire the Negroes to do nothing, not unless they're out on the farm or something. And you know, SCLC, they probably start protesting for better jobs, something like that, and the Negro could come from the bottom towards the top, if he don't make it to the top.

— Would you join the protest?

Yeah, I would.

— What do you think about violence to bring about changes?

I don't think you have to use violence to bring about change. You know, I think you can go to a person and talk to 'em, and some way you can get over to 'em, and then after you talk so long and he still don't seem to understand what you talking about, probably bring about violence then. But actually I don't go for it.

— So you think the problems of this country can be solved without violence.

No, naw, not in this part of the country. You know, I think the only way it gon change here, you gon have to have a little violence, somebody gon have to do something or nuther. They not gon change that easily.

— What do you think most whites around here think of national Negro advances?

On the whole around here, you might find two or three white men that think Negroes should have advances. Because we have two Negro policemen, and I imagine if they was to lock up too many white men, they'd get fired. They wouldn't have 'em up there.

— What did you think about the "Black Power" slogan?

What I think about black power? Actually, I think black power is where a big group of Negroes all work together and they pull the same way each time for the same thing. And mostly with black power they have to get mostly everything they want, if they have any power.

— Do you think that's a good thing?

Yeah . . . Actually, it's been a long time since I heard black power, because I think if all the Negroes feel the same as I do, I would want to be integrated sooner or later.

— Would you want to be separate and have power?

No. I ain't got no need for being different from anybody else. I wanna be the same.

— Who was your favorite president?

It was President Kennedy. Actually, I believe that's the reason he was assassinated, he was trying to help the Negroes too, these poor Negroes. And then, I reckon, the white man in power didn't like it because he was trying to help us. That's the reason he was assassinated.

— What do you think of Lester Maddox?

You know he didn't even get a high school education, he's a high school dropout. So if a Negro was to go up there to try to run for governor who was a high school dropout, I don't even believe they'd let him run myself.

— What do you think of politicians in this area?

All the politicians in this area is run by the white man, so they got all the advantages they need over the Negro, see. Actually, the way they is, the Negroes in this part won't vote for nothing. But still they want the Negroes up in front. They want to be up on top, they want to be up with the white, but come time to register and vote they won't do it. And then after the whites elect someone, they'll be standing out mumbling, talking about they didn't want him. But they won't go up there and register to vote for theirself.

See, I think if the Negro really want to be a citizen, they should vote. At election time you hardly ever see a Negro person vote. They had this registration drive here, they was trying to go around and tell all the Negroes to register and vote. Most of 'em in town, I think they did. But out in the country, not none of them voted. Wasn't no Negroes got into office. But I believe if all the Negroes was to go up there and vote, something gon happen and the white man will be back there in the chair again. See, something's wrong with the voting in Adamsville. I believe that actually last time when they was voting for city commission, I believe that a Negro won then.

No, my parents ain't registered. Actually, I tell 'em. But most of the time they get angry if you tell 'em about it. You know, I tell 'em they should go up there and register to vote because, like I said, if someone is elected and they don't want 'em, they'll start talking. But if they had gone up there and registered to vote theirself it probably would have turned out a different way. But, you know, my parents, they tell you, "You ain't got nothing to do with me," something like that.

•　　•　　•

The law around here, they're all right now. See, about three years ago, my brother-in-law, he was riding through Adamsville and the main police stopped him. The policeman took him to jail and told him he could call his bossman to go his bond. But then he wouldn't let him call him, and so my brother-in-law started going across the street — that's where his bossman lived — and the policeman beat him up. Knocked holes all in his head, had to get stitches. Did it with a blackjack.

After the policeman beat him up, he went inside the jailhouse and locked himself in. You know, the streets and everything was full; most every Negro in Adamsville was up there. So when my brother-in-law got back there, the policeman was inside the jail locked in so couldn't nobody get in where he was. He was just in there by himself. He stayed in there all that night until the next day. And then he opened the door and let the sheriff in, and he brought him out.

And about last year he killed a Negro man. Man was driving a trailer truck, he stopped him. They say they exchanged a few words, and the policeman told him to get out of the truck, so when the man opened the door to get out, the policeman shot him. And then the dead man's wife sued the policeman. And he been going straight ever since then.

•　　•　　•

For fun, I like to play basketball. Dancing, and socializing with young ladies.

Mostly, we go out there to the grill. I go there about twice a month. Most of the time I be here getting my lessons. No, I don't drink at the grill. I don't drink no ways. See, after these people get drunk they go to clowning and going on. If they get drunk and go home and get in bed or something like that, that'd be another thing. But the way they be acting in the street, it look bad, and especially a young boy being drunk. I don't dig it.

— Do you ever go to Columbus?

No, I don't hardly ever go to Columbus. It's because of transportation mostly. I would like to go more often if I had the transportation. See, my brother lets me use his car and when I get his car I go down quite often. I go to movies.

The best movie I saw was *The Lost Man* with Sidney Poitier. See, when it first started, he had a big group of men, they was going into this government building. They were trying to get some money. See, all these poor people, poor Negro people, they was in this town. And see, he wanted to get 'em money and stuff so they could buy food and clothing because the white peoples, they wouldn't let 'em work. I like the way he was trying to help the poor people like that. He got caught. He had gotten this white girlfriend, and they killed both of 'em.

Yeah, we got a TV. On Tuesday night I watch it. "Room 222" and "Mod Squad" — I watch those two pictures. See, there's this girl on "Room 222," I like to watch her, the way she be acting. And on "Mod Squad" I just like the way those three young cops act when they work.

•　　•　　•

The most exciting thing ever happened to me is when I first got my driver's license. I passed my written test but I never had no car to take the driving test in. Finally, I used a friend of mine's. Another boy and I went the same day to take the written test. See, he dropped out of school when he was round about thirteen years old. He couldn't read too good so me and him went the same day. It was a lot of peoples up there and all of us were sitting at a table together, and he was sitting right beside me and I was showing him how to do his questions. So we both made the same thing on the test. So the man came and asked me, "Y'all didn't do no copying, did you?" I said, "No, I didn't."

Something else real exciting was one Saturday night about two years ago my sister gave me a surprise birthday party. She lives in Atlanta and she came home that Saturday morning and she told me to come home after I got off from work. So after I got off from work I came on home. About 8:30 I came up to the house, and the house was full! All my girlfriends and everybody was here. I walked in the door and almost fainted. When I walked in the house everybody

was real quiet. She had a long table down the hall and chairs at the table and a
big chicken.

•   •   •

— What's your favorite daydream?

Mostly these girls. Sometimes I sitting there thinking about 'em. It's real
funny. A girl, you know, she real smart; you know, they wanna be. You can see
her doing something and then she'll swear to God she was doing something else.
Some of 'em, they nice to be around. But again — whooh! — whole lot of trouble
sometimes.

I don't know, but a girl, she's real nice, some of 'em. She give you that certain feeling. Some of 'em give you the feeling you wanna marry 'em but . . . It's
a real strong feeling. See, she get to talking to you; you know, she tell you that
she looking for her man to settle down with her. Says she don't wanna run around
all her life, looking for a man. You know, something like that. It make you wanna
settle down, but study about it for a while and it just go away.

— Have you had many girlfriends?

Felton Jones   81

Yeah, I've had quite a few girlfriends. I had some of 'em, you know, they was real nice, but, boy, some of 'em, I swear — kind of tough. Like one I met in Florida. I met her in the street and talked to her about thirty minutes and then she asked me to marry her. I hadn't even been to her home or nothing. At first I thought she was just kidding, jiving around, saying I'll marry you. But pretty soon I realized she was serious, and I left.

— What do you look for in a girl?

First, if I see a girl and I see does she act real nice, you know, and see how she carry herself, and then you know she don't act that wild — you know some girls act wild and just throw theirself away. They just get out and go and you see 'em in the street anytime at night, you know, they be drinking and going on. I don't care too much about that. I be looking for those nice girls.

I got two or three girlfriends now. I'm not going with just one. See, if you go with one of 'em, she ain't gon do right, you got to get two or three, you know.

Now, I had this one girl named Judy; I think . . . well, yeah, I was in love with her. I met her one night when my sister give me a surprise birthday party. That Saturday evening when they brought me home, everybody was here. My brother gave me a drink machine — he worked for a meat-packing company and he got it there. They had it sitting out there. So I was going out there where the machine was and I saw this girl standing out there. So when I get there — she knowed my brother because she used to work in the peach orchard with him — she said, "Hey, ain't you Richard's brother?" I said, "Yeah." So she kept on talking.

You know, at first I didn't pay her too much attention at the time because a lot of people here. So I left and came back in the house and then she came in, so I started talking to her again. So we stand there a long time talking. So I asked her could I take her home. She told me yeah, so I took her home.

She was a real nice girl and she knew how to carry herself, and, I don't know, I reckon she was crazy about me. And she just became a part of me. And I was real crazy about her, but when I left last summer I didn't see her for three months so I guess I just forgot about her. See, during the summer, I think she went to Florida or somewhere, so when I came back to see her she was gone. So I said she's gone, might as well forget about her, you know. See, she didn't say nothing about she was leaving or nothing, she just was gone. And then I came back home the Fourth of July, so I saw her then. We both went to this party and everything, but I saw then after she had been gone, I didn't like her too much. Just forgot about her.

Actually, I was crazy about her, but when we broke up, you know, it was

... I think about it right now, it hurts you sometimes to think about it. But she real nice to me and I just forgot about her. She call me now, sometime, at night. Want to talk to me. I think it's about time to go back together again. I was talking to her last night and she told me she was real lonely so she need somebody to talk to over the phone. So I told her, "There's some other little boys looking for a nice lady like you." But, you know, actually, I was just trying to cheer her up. I think I'll make it back with her sometime. Before the week's out.

• • •

— Do you want to get married and have children someday?

Not hardly. If I do it'll be a pretty good while, you know, about ten or twenty years. You know, I don't want to get involved too much before I have a good time. Then I probably get old and settle down then.

If I had kids, I wouldn't want but a couple of 'em. I don't want no big family, I want just a couple of kids. So I can take care of 'em. Actually, I don't know how it would be about ten or fifteen years from now. I don't know whether you be making more money ... But I imagine if you be making more money, the prices go up and still you be in the same fix as now. But if I could do like what I plan to do, you know, I think I'll have a pretty good job for supporting kids.

• • •

— Suppose you could be born as somebody else. Who would you like to be?

I probably want to be Dr. Martin Luther King. Because I like what he was trying to do for the poor Negro and that he was trying, you know, to march for their rights.

— Would you like to do like he did yourself?

Yeah, I'd like to do that myself, because so many Negroes ... some of 'em —
I know I'm like that myself — kind of poor, ain't got nothing. But some of 'em, they real poorer than I am. For instance, this lady that live right here in Adamsville, right here on the corner, she got these kids and they real dirty and all that. I think she need help with 'em. She probably getting help with 'em, but whatever she getting she probably must not get enough. I'd try to get her enough money so she could get her a home, because there she don't even have a door, she have a little rag up to the door. And try to help her to get her kids some clothes to wear because they be barefooted the year round.

— Have you ever thought of doing things like Dr. King did?

Yeah, uh-huh. I thought if I could just get involved, you know, in uh ...
See, you have to have someone to be in the background, you just can't go by

yourself, the way I figure it. But if I could get somebody to go with me, you know, to stand up with me — I can stand up alone but I need somebody to stand with me. Most teen-agers, they're scared or something, I don't know. Kind of scared.

You know, it's a group of boys in Pineville, they're scared in a way; they talk about it, but I don't think they do too much about it. Talk about getting what they want, you know. Most places around here a Negro have to go in the back to get something to eat. So one day Mr. East, our white teacher we have at school, he was telling us about he don't think that's right for a Negro to go in the back to get something to eat. Says his money just as good as a white man's.

But, anyway, the kids in Pineville, they came down here to this restaurant where we was, and they was telling some of us in the back they was *going in the front*. And if they told 'em to go to the back, they told us what they gon do — said they was gon turn it out, you know, just start tearing the place up. We were just talking about it.

— Were you going to do it with them?

Yeah. I was with 'em, but most of 'em, they just like to jive around, they wasn't serious or nothing.

— Were you serious about it?

Yeah, I was serious about it. But, no, can't go by myself. Because if I just go there by myself, they'd probably have me locked up or something like that. I know mostly they would. The police and things, they're out for us. They don't want you to come in that front to eat, I know that much. But it's the same way at the State Patrol Headquarters at Manchester. They don't want a Negro to come in the front, have a sign say "Colored." One sign say "Colored" and the other sign don't say what.

— How do you feel about not being able to go into the front of restaurants?

I don't never go in a place like that.

— If you wanted something to eat, would you go in the back?

No, I'd try the front first. If I couldn't get nothing in the front, I wouldn't eat at all. The reason I wouldn't go to the back because mostly they keep animals and things in the back, make you feel like you a dog or something, you know, going around to the back to eat, don't want you to associate with the white people or something like that. I don't like it.

•　　•　　•

— If you could be born as somebody else, who would you definitely not want to be?

I wouldn't want to be Cassius Clay. After the draft, he had to pay all that

money out. I dig his style of fighting, but after they called him to the Army I figured he should of went on instead of paying all that money out to dodge it. I was kind of with him. He didn't know what he was fighting for, wasn't no need for him to go over there to fight. But then there's two sides to it. If everybody else had to go, I think he should of went too.

I don't know what I think of the war. It's kind of hard to say. I be like Clay about the war because I don't know what I be fighting for. I reckon after I got there I could go shoot, just go kill a man for no reason, but it be kind of hard to do. I don't have no idea what they're fighting for. I think about it a lot. You know, mostly all the boys around here go to Viet Nam and I ask questions about how the war is and what they be fighting for, but everybody that come back, they don't know what they fighting for. But they tell you how it is. Some of 'em say they like it and some of 'em say they don't want no part of it.

· · ·

The worst thing that ever happened to me . . . It got to be when they took my license. They took it last year. I was in Atlanta and had an accident; a man ran in back of me and I ain't got no insurance. They transferred the case from Atlanta down here, and so I went to court down here. So they asked me what happened, I told 'em, and then the judge took my license for a year. I always didn't know what was going on, they just took my license, I reckon just because there wasn't nobody in the courthouse but me and the judge and about three or four other white men. At first, Judge Lee, he didn't even say nothing about taking my license. Another white man got up and he told the judge, say, "Judge Lee, I think you should take his license." So the judge told me he gon keep my license for three months.

I went back up there when three months was up, and then they told me the judge — he's from Columbus — wouldn't be back in town before next year. And so when I got it back, it was a whole year that I didn't have my license. And actually they took my license for nothing, because when somebody runs into the back of you, automatically it's his fault.

· · ·

— What in life gives you the most satisfaction?

The romantic part, the romance part. I don't know why, I don't know. It's real exciting. You know, just talking and, you know . . .

· · ·

— Have you ever wished you were someone else?

Yeah, sometimes. Actually, when I wish I was someone else is when I want something and don't have the money to get it with. So I think of someone who got a lot of money, something like that, really fixed up for theirself. I wish I was fixed up like them. White and Negro. It's the white most of the time because they the ones that got most of the money.

— Do you wish you were white?

No, I don't wish I was white, but I wish I had some of the money they have.

And at times I wish that I was Sidney Poitier. Because, you know, the money he make and a Negro, he's a real good actress, I sort of like him.

•   •   •

What do I want out of life? I want a good job, and a home, I wanna live happy. And you know, after I get a good job and a home, I wouldn't want anybody coming around and disturbing me or anything. I just wanna be by myself.

— What do you mean someone disturbing you?

Well, what I mean by somebody disturbing you, where someone comes around . . . For instance, the insurance people, someone come around like that collecting money. I just don't want 'em ever coming around because it get kind of aggravating at times. The way it is now, most of the time they come to your house on Sunday and if you not at home, they'll come to the church. I don't go for that. Because if I'm gon pay 'em, I'll pay 'em at home. And I'm not going to pay 'em on Sunday no way. Like there was this man — yeah, he was white — that sold Dixie Auto Insurance, he come to church all the time collecting money. That's the reason I didn't take out any insurance this year. See, he kept coming to the church, come out there and blow his horn, someone goes out there and see what he wants, he tell 'em he wanna see me. And I didn't go for it.

•   •   •

— What has been your biggest problem in growing up?

Trying to get out of school is my biggest problem. I wanna get out so bad . . . The time is drawing near, and actually, I'm doing pretty good. I think I'll make it though.

Janice Riley

*Sixteen-year-old Janice Riley lives with her grandmother, bed-ridden grand-
father, and little sister in a small, lopsided house in the squalid "colored section"
of Bradford, Georgia. Her manner is apathetic, although on occasion her mood
unexpectedly brightens. She usually talks listlessly in a very low voice, even when
expressing hostility; her tone often borders on despair.*

— What are some of your first memories?

I remember when I used to stay with my mother and get a whipping every
day. I stayed with her until I was four years old and got whipped just about
every day. I was pretty bad. Because once I cut my brother. We was playing
playhouse and my mother called him upstairs and when he went up there, I called
him downstairs to play. He wouldn't hurry up and come, so I got me a cut piece
of glass to cut him with. He wouldn't come to see what I want, so when he did
come I cut him.

— Do you have any happy childhood memories?

Huh-uh.

— You weren't happy?

I wasn't that happy, I don't believe, because I got a whipping every day. I
wasn't that happy.

•   •   •

When I was small I used to have some epileptic fits or something. I started having 'em when I was four. When I was nine or ten or something, I went to the hospital in Columbus and stayed there. The last time I had a fit, I think it was '64. And I go in there sometimes for a checkup now. I don't know nothing about the fits because my mama would say I would blank out. Can't remember nothing.

•   •   •

I been living with my grandmother since I was four. My mother lives right up the road. I don't know why I came to live with my grandmother. I think I came down here to take care of my granddaddy while my grandmother works — she's a midwife, always off helping birth babies, and she helps out at a white lady's house on Fridays. My granddaddy, he has arthritis; he been in bed for about fourteen years.

Me and my sister — she's seven — we both live here with my grandmother. I got eight more brothers and sisters live with my mother. And I got a brother that live in New York and two sisters in New Jersey and another brother that live around here.

— Tell me about your brothers and sisters.

Well, I'll start with my brother Jonathan. He's twenty-two and he lives in New York. He's okay, but . . . Well, he's okay, I think, since he married. Before that when he lived down here he went to jail every Saturday night. Put in jail for fighting every Saturday night. The last time he was in jail . . . I think it was last year. Yeah, they beat up the white policeman, him and another brother, Fletcher. The policeman, Cal Jones, he kind of cripple. They didn't like him for something, so they got him behind the café one night and beat him. And then they told him not to tell . . . He had them all put in jail. I don't know why they did it. They just go for bad mostly.

And Fletcher, he twenty-one, he live around here. He always taking up for me, and so is Tommy. He's seventeen. Like if I get in an argument with somebody, I just call them and they come and beat him up. Like one time my friend and I was at school and this guy Donald, he walked up. He told me, "Come here." I told him, "Go ahead," because I didn't want to talk to him and he slapped me and then Tommy told him don't hit me no more. Then Donald and his twin brother grabbed my brother. Then I went and called Fletcher, Fletcher came over and, wow, he had a real fight.

And Napoleon, he just twelve or thirteen, he like to play a lot. Let's see, I have one more brother, Freddie. I like him because he not but ten and we always get to fighting, but I still like him. And then, I got another brother, but

he dead. He was immature when he was born; you know, he was not fully developed. He was about one or two when he died.

Let's see, now I start my sisters. The oldest one, when I was two, she left to Jersey and I didn't get to know her too much. And Peggy — she's another one — she twenty and she live in Jersey. And Becky, she's thirteen, she okay because we more like sisters. And then I got another one, eleven, and she wild and, boy, I don't like her that much. And Vivian, the one that stay here, she okay, but she too skinny. And Rosetta, she's six, she okay, but she's real mean. And Julia, she like to fight a lot; and Amelia, the baby, she like to play around and eat a lot, like I do — I always like to eat all the time. And that's fourteen.

— Are all of your brothers and sisters your full brothers and sisters?

No, it just five of them my whole brothers and sisters and the rest is half. My five oldest brothers and sisters is half, and my two youngest is half.

All of 'em is my mother's children. She been married twice. She separated from her first husband before I was born, I think, and then she got married to my father, and then they separated in '66, and he died in 1967. And the other children, she had by another man she not married to — Bud Hudson, and she still be with him a lot now. And she got another baby coming in June.

— Have you ever seen her first husband?

Yes, I see him during the summer. And I seen him when he came to get my sister and I seen him once before when his mother died when he came over here. He real nice.

— Did your mother and he not get along?

No, because she always shooting at him. She was shooting at him every weekend, I believe, with a shotgun. She wasn't trying to kill him, I don't think. That's what she always tells my brothers. She always joking them about it and how they used to cry when she used to shoot at him.

— Tell me about your father.

My daddy, he was the nicest person I knew. He bought me everything I ever wanted, and he didn't want nobody to mess with me or hit me or anything. That's about all.

— Was he like that with all the children?

No, just me mostly. Why? I guess because I didn't never talk back to him like my other brothers and sisters.

— Did he have any bad points to you?

Well, he drank for one. Not much, but he just get drunk on weekends. He just come home, lay down, and go to sleep.

— He wasn't loud or mean or anything?

I'm Somebody Important

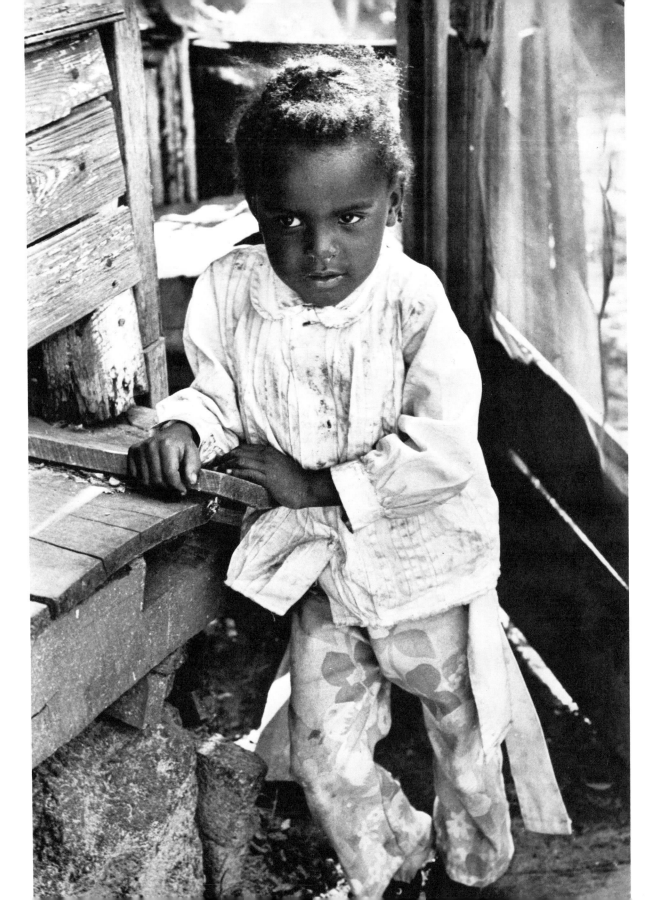

If I kind of mess with him, he probably was. Like, mostly every time he get drunk, I go and ask him for some money and he always gave me some, and then he probably holler at me, like that, that's all.

— How did he and your mother get along?

Okay. They didn't fight.

— Did they argue?

Yeah, sometimes. About me. Everything I wanted my mother wouldn't give it to me, but my daddy wanted me to have it. Like I want something like candy or a dress or something and my daddy said I could get it, she wouldn't let me have it, said I had too much already. Then they always argue about something like that.

— How did you feel when your father died?

Well, I didn't believe it at first. They said he was dead. Then I realized he was dead then, I just . . . I don't know. At first I felt kind of funny and then it was all right, I don't know.

— How did you find out he had died?

I was at work up at the café, and my stepmother called me; see, he had got married again. She called me and told me to call my mother. So I called my mother and she told me I was telling her a lie. She just hung up because she said I was telling her a lie. But then she found out.

— Why did she think you were telling a lie?

Because I always used to call her and tell her something stupid. Like I just called her and pretend I'm my little sister, and tell her my brother said something, like that. I just call her and tell her my brother Jonathan's coming home or he got a baby, something like that.

— Why did you do that?

I don't know, just to hear her fuss, I guess.

— Do you like your mother?

Yeah, I like her.

— Why didn't you call her and talk about something else?

I don't know. I guess I was just stupid.

— Is Bud Hudson, the man your mother goes with now, married?

No.

— How do you feel about him?

I *hate* him. He's too fresh. Every time I see him, he always trying to feel on me or something, so I don't like him. I tell my mama about it and I tell my brothers, my brothers gon beat him up.

— How do you feel about your mother going with him?

I get real mad mostly. I argue her about it. I tell her she don't need her old man because I don't like him, none of the kids like him. I just be telling her she don't need him and she get mad and tell me what I don't need.

— How did you feel when she had her first baby by him?

I got mad, real mad. I fussed at her a whole lot; I fussed at her till I turned red, I believe. That's the maddest I ever got, I think. I told her she do it again, I gon kill her.

— How did you feel when she had another baby by him?

I told her if she had another one, I wasn't gon take care of him. I was gon throw him outdoors and dare anybody to go get him. She don't believe I really meant it, but I do, because I don't . . . I don't like it.

— What are your mother's good points?

Well, let's see, ever since my daddy died, she gives me mostly everything I want. That's probably all. Oh, yeah, and when I have F on my report card, she don't say nothing but I better get it off.

— What are her bad points?

Bad? I don't know. Oh, she don't want me to go with certain guys I wanna go with and that all. She just picked out a couple of 'em she didn't want me to go with, and most of 'em she picked out were the ones I was going with. But I'm not going with 'em now. She said they was bad. Most of 'em go to jail every weekend like Fletcher used to. They mostly go to jail for fighting, stealing, or something. They probably break in the schoolhouse or come around and go break in somebody's house or something.

— Have you ever stolen anything?

Yeah, I stole an egg Easter Sunday. From my grandmother. See, she left me here to take care of my grandfather while she go to work. She told me I could eat the egg when I get ready, but I had just finished eating breakfast, I think. And then when she left, I told my granddaddy I wasn't gon eat nothing, and then I went into the house and slipped me the egg outdoors and ate it. Then my gum hopped up — it have a big knot on it now — and I won't steal nothing else.

— In what ways do you think you're different from your mother?

All the ways, I guess. I don't know how I'm different. I guess because I like to eat a lot and she don't. And my mama like to work and I don't. She works at the peanut sheller, pick the trash from the peanuts.

— You don't like to work?

No, rather do nothing. I don't know why, I guess I'm just lazy.

— Do you ever do anything fun with your mother?

Yeah, I play ball mostly with my mama. We play softball and we pitch and hit the ball and everything. I don't even like it that much, but I do it because she want to sometime. She told me I need some exercise. I reckon because I lay around and eat all the time and that's all.

•   •   •

— Have you ever wanted to leave home?

Yeah, I think it was this morning; no, it was yesterday, either one. I don't like for nobody to holler at me, and my mama, and Fletcher, they was hollering at me. And they tell me they like to holler at me and I tell them I'm gon leave them and never come back and everything. And most of the time I be meaning it.

— Have you ever seriously thought about leaving?

Yeah. It's been a long time ago, I don't know what I did to make my grandmother mad. And mostly when my sister used to beat me all the time, I talk about leaving then. And one time I packed my clothes and they're still packed. I packed 'em last summer when I first came home from Jersey; see, last summer I stayed with my sister in Jersey. I don't know why I was mad. I think mostly because my grandmother told me to come home before the twenty-fifth and I didn't want to come home *until* the twenty-fifth. So when I came home I unpacked my clothes, and then we got to fussing about it. And then I packed my clothes back up, say I was gon leave and I ain't never gon come back.

— And your clothes are still packed?

Yeah, I look in the suitcase and get them out to wear now.

— Why haven't you unpacked them?

I don't know, I keep on thinking about leaving, I guess.

•   •   •

— If you could make wishes for your mother and grandmother that would come true, what would they be?

For my mother, that she could move in her own house, and that's about all. And for my grandmother, a trailer, like she always wanted. She been saying a trailer would be nice, said she gon get her one day.

— Would you rather live here in your house or in a trailer?

I'd rather live in a trailer than live here most of the time because I wouldn't have to clean up so much. Because there wouldn't be so many beds, I don't think, or so many clothes and so much junk and everything. And we would have all gas and no wood, all gas or either electric and no wood, and then I wouldn't have to tote any more wood, wouldn't have to cut none, or nothing like that.

•   •   •

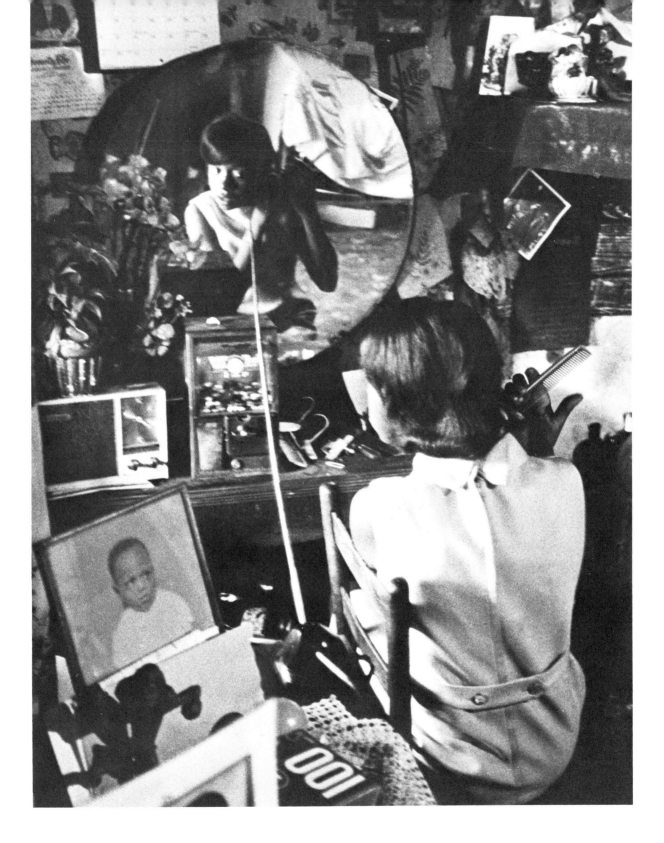

— Do you wish you had more or fewer brothers and sisters?

More brothers and less sisters. I wish I had more brothers so they could fight for me and give me some money all the time.

• • •

— What do you usually do after school?

Eat, and walk the streets, and watch TV, and come down here and lay down and look at the wall. I do that all the time, just come down here and look at that wall or the top of the house.

— Why do you do that?

I don't know, I don't have nothing else to do.

— Do you like to do it?

Some of the time. I just come down here and think about things. Mostly I think about my tests and how I'm doing in school, and wonder if I'm going to the twelfth grade next year, and I think about Wally. He's my boyfriend.

— What do you do when you walk the streets?

Just walk around and look around.

— What do you think about?

Nothing, just be walking.

— Do you like to do that?

Not all the time, but I don't have anything else to do.

— What do you like to do?

What do I like to do? Eat.

— Do you feel happy when you eat?

Yeah.

— What have you eaten in the hour since you've been home from school?

I been eating a whole lot of foolishness. I ate a orange, some cake, a honeybun, I drank a soda, and had a banana and some candy.

— What do you usually have for supper?

We usually have collard greens for supper, but I hardly ever eat it; I eat mostly cake and ice cream.

— Do you usually have meat for supper?

No, because most of the meat we have I can't eat it, because every time I eat a whole lot of greasy food, I throw it back up.

— You don't like meat?

Well, I like hamburgers and hotdogs. I like sweets.

— Do things ever get boring in Bradford?

No, I always have something to do. There's not much to do around here,

I'm Somebody Important

but I can find something, like go to the café before they said teen-agers couldn't go there no more or go worry my mama some.

— How do you worry your mother?

Try to get some money out of her.

— So do you like it in Bradford?

A little. I just like the town and be around my friends.

— What do you not like about it?

There's not many people here. I like to be around a lot of people all the time, I don't know why. And there's too many peanut things around here. Everybody works for peanuts. Too many buildings for peanuts and all that.

— What do you not like about that?

Well, see, the way it used to be, it used to be houses and places for young people to go. Like there was a building where we could go and have fun, have

Janice Riley

a jukebox and everything. Then Jim Johnson have them tore down and put peanut warehouses up. See, Jim Johnson own just about everything, all the houses and everything and all the peanut warehouses and things.

— How do people around here feel about Jim Johnson?

Most of the older people like him, but the younger ones, I don't think they like him too much. I know that I just don't like him. He always have his way with everything, get everything, and I don't like him.

— How do you feel about that?

I don't like it, but nothing I can do about it . . . Not yet.

— What all does he get his way about?

Like moving people out their homes and tearing 'em down so he can put up a peanut warehouse, or moving their houses so they can have the place where the house was for Century Village, this place they're making for tourists down here. Moved my mother twice. He moved her out in '67 and '69. Moved her whole house in '69; she was renting it from him, and they still live in it. He moved it so they could have the place for Century Village.

And in '67, he tore that house down, so he could put up his peanut sheller. He came and told her that they'd have to move. He gave her, I think, a week. And then she and all the kids stayed here at my grandmother's until she could find a house. They stayed here about six months.

— How did your mother feel about having to move?

I don't think she liked it . . . Oh, she was gon move anyway because four families lived in the same house. She wanted her some room, enough rooms; she didn't have but two rooms then, and she had ten kids. And when Jim Johnson told her in '69 they was gon move her house, she said they was gon buy them a home to stay, won't have to move no more.

— How did you feel about their having to move twice?

It didn't bother me. It didn't bother me because the first time when they stayed here until she found another house, I had more sisters here with me and then I wouldn't be scared to go through the house. See, my brother told me my daddy gon get me or a haint [ghost] or something gon get me, and I be scared. Told me a haint gon get me or my daddy, one.

— Do you think of this very often?

Every day. I'm scared. Tommy, my brother, he always scare me at night. He always come knock on the door when he think ain't nobody here but me and my granddaddy, or either go around to the back door and knock on the door and pretend he a haint or something. And I'm scared something gon get me.

No, I haven't never seen one, but I thought I saw two eyes coming at me last night. I was in the kitchen taking a bath. But it was just a cat peeping through the door.

— Do you believe your father would ever come back and haint you?

I *don't know*. I don't think so, though. He might and he might not.

— Why do you think your father might come back and haint you?

Because whenever he tell me to do something I wouldn't do it, I guess. Like I go where he be working at and I be worrying him about some money, trying to get some money out of him, and he tell me to go on. But I wouldn't do it, I'd go sit in his car about two or three hours.

•　　•　　•

— Do you ever go to Columbus to see movies?

No. But I saw some movies last summer in Jersey when I was staying with my sister. I saw three of 'em I really like. One of 'em, *The Cats*, I like it because there was this girl, she came into see this boy's aunt and she wanted to get some money out of her. And she was gon kill this lady for her money, but the girl ended up dying herself because of these cats that made her fall off a ladder.

And *Johnny, I Love You*, I like that one because it was about black peoples, most of it. It was happening on the day they buried Martin Luther King and this guy named Johnny got some other guys and they went to this warehouse to get these guns and they was gon have a war against the white peoples. But Johnny, he got caught and they kilt him. I just liked it because Johnny, he was a nice-looking guy.

— Did you think what he was doing was a good idea?

No. I don't think they should have tried to have a war against the white people; they should have tried to talk it out or something, I don't know.

— Do you think talking would do any good?

Some of the time it will, most of the time it won't. Because I try to talk to some people, like my friends; it don't do no good, I end up fighting. Like I had one about two weeks ago with my friend, Sally. Oh, brother, she's my worst enemy; she think I go with her boyfriend J.B. See, she came down here, gon beat up my little sister. She wanted to get revenge on me, I guess; I don't know. Me and her boyfriend got into an argument and she got mad about it. He get jealous of me talking to a whole lot of guys and things and so he got mad and just called me a whore, and I told him his sister and his girlfriend was one. And then he got mad about it, and then she got mad, and she came down here to beat up my sister, and I wasn't gon let her. So she got mad at me and wanted to fight about it. I tried to talk to her about it but she wouldn't listen for nothing. I just told her

I wasn't mad with her or nothing like that and she told me she was gon beat me, and I told her I was ready for her. So we had a fight.

.　　.　　.

— Who's your best friend?

I don't have a best friend.

— Do you have any good friends?

Yeah. Lucille Higgins and Rebecca Holland. I like them because they nice and better than other girls. They like to talk a lot and eat a lot like I do, and most other girls, they hang around boys.

— Why don't you like to hang around boys?

Just haven't thought about boys, not that much. They're okay but I wouldn't like to hang around 'em all the time.

— Do you get along well with most people?

No. Because the girls around here, they just hate me, that's all. Mostly everyone I see around town hates me. They say I try to take their boyfriends or something like that. They always tell me I always go around and try to take other girls' boyfriends or — I don't know what all they tell me. And I have more boys that's friends than they do. Most every boy that come into town, he's my friend, they don't even know him and I won't introduce him to 'em or something.

— Do you try to take away boyfriends?

No. Huh-uh. I just don't be interested in these boys in Bradford. I don't know why. It's just knowing 'em, and I been around 'em mostly all my life, and — huh-uh.

— Why do they think you try to take their boyfriends away?

I don't know, I guess because I'm always smiling at 'em.

— Why do you do that?

I don't know, it's just something I can't help.

— Does it upset you not to have more girlfriends?

No. Except when I be out on Saturday nights, because I have no one to talk to unless it's some stupid boy. Like when we used to go to the café I'd always be there by myself most of the time unless'n Tommy come over and sit with me. Just sit there by myself and watch the other people go by. Most of the time I don't mind because I'd rather be there by myself so I can think about Wally.

.　　.　　.

Wally's my boyfriend. He's a soldier, he at Fort Jackson.

— Tell me a little about him.

Janice Riley

He's . . . I don't know, he's undescribable. He's tall and kind of bright and got a big bush. I don't know that much about him. I met him in '68 at the café. He's from Columbus, and they was in Bradford playing ball against my brother and them. I was working at the café, and he asked me to fix them a cheeseburger, and my brother introduced me to him.

— What is it you like about him?

Well, he's just real nice, about the nicest person I ever met. And he just better than other boys I met.

— When you think about Wally while you look at the wall and while you're alone at the café, what do you think about?

Marrying Wally. I think about where we'll live and stuff like that. How many kids we'll have, and how we'll be, whether he be mean or something like that.

— Do you think he might be mean?

Well, he not mean now. I don't know.

— Do you think people change when they get married?

Most of 'em, they do. They get worse. Boy, the women have a boyfriend on every street. And I don't like it in a way because I don't think they're treating their husbands fair.

— Would you go out on your husband?

No.

— Do you think your husband would go out on you?

He probably would.

— What would you do?

I'd probably shoot him. No, huh-uh. I'd probably talk it over first. And then I might call my brother and let him beat him up a couple of times.

— You said you daydreamed about where you and Wally would live . . .

Yeah, mostly New York or Washington. And our house be kind of big, about five bedrooms and upstairs. And have nice furniture.

— Do you and Wally make out much?

No, Wally's never kissed me.

•　　•　　•

I got four boyfriends. They Wally, Ted . . . Ted was stationed at Fort Benning. And J.B. tries to be my boyfriend. And the other one's Jim, he was in the Army but he's out now.

— Do you go out with all of them?

No, just Wally when he's home, and Jim.

— Tell me about Jim.

Well, he lives over in Hendersonville; that's about ten miles away. And one time he asked me to marry him, I was real excited. He was in Germany and I was in Bradford and he asked me to marry him. Shoot, I got happy over it and then I thought about it and I didn't want him.

— Why?

I don't want nobody from Bradford or Hendersonville.

— You say you felt happy about it.

Yeah, at first. I felt happy because I was gon leave home, and then I thought about it and thought it wouldn't be no better, so I changed my mind.

— Do you like him a lot?

No, I don't like him.

— Do you like Wally a lot?

Yeah.

— Do you think you're in love with him?

I don't know . . . No.

— Have you ever been in love?

No.

— Do you think you ever will be?

I don't think so, my brother told me I won't. He said I try to keep too many boys at one time.

— Why did he say that?

Because every time a new guy come along, I get him.

— Think you'll always be like that?

No, because I planning on leaving one day.

— Why will that make a difference?

I'm planning on going in the Army, and I won't be falling for them then, I don't think.

— Why not?

It just be too many just to pick over one or two.

•   •   •

— What would you like to do in the Army?

Well, mostly help out at a desk or help wounded soldiers out. I'd like to go to Viet Nam. I want to because I just want to go so I can — well, I might find my old boyfriend over there.

— What about Wally?

Well, I don't know, because I can forget him.

— Who is the old boyfriend you want to find?

Edward Carver. Met him at my mama's house. One Sunday I got home from church and my brother and some more guys was there, and Edward was up there and my oldest brother introduced me to him, and about two months later he left for Viet Nam. I really liked him, yeah.

— What made you want to go in the Army?

Well, last year we had some entertainment at school and we had some Navy people to talk to us and some Army mens to come to the school to talk about it and tell us how it is. And so they gave me the idea.

— Do you think you *will* go in the Army?

I don't think so. I just don't think so right now. I don't know why; I guess I want Wally and I don't want Wally . . . If I go in the Army I won't get him, and if I don't go in the Army I'll probably get him. See, Wally told me if I go in the Army, he might not want me when I get back.

— Which would you rather have, Wally or the Army?

Wally.

· · ·

— No matter who you end up marrying, what kind of person would you like your husband to be?

He have to be nice and he have to be tall. And probably talk a lot and eat a lot, because I do. And kind of dark. And he have to finish school. I don't want a dropout, because it be hard for a dropout to get a job.

— Do you want to get married?

Yeah.

— Would you want to have children?

Yeah. I'd want about six probably.

— Do you think you'll end up marrying Wally?

I probably would. He says he'll marry me after I get out of school. I don't know if I'll marry him right then, I probably will.

— As soon as you get out of school?

No . . . I don't know, he probably be dead by then. I don't know. He's going to Viet Nam.

— Do you think he might be killed?

I hope not. I don't think he will get killed. My first boyfriend got killed in Viet Nam.

— Who was that?

Edward. Edward Carver. He got killed over a year ago. We started going together about two months before he went over to Viet Nam.

— How did you feel when you learned he was dead?

I was upset. I don't know, I was real upset. Because he told me he could take care of hisself. And, well, he volunteered for the Army, I can say that much. I don't know . . . Because the next day I found another soldier. I guess I . . . I don't know.

— Did you like him as much as Wally?

More, I think.

— Do you think Wally loves you?

He say he do. That's all I go by, he say he do.

— Do you love him?

A little.

— What do you mean by a little?

Well, I have other things outside of him on my mind right now, and I don't know. I'm worrying about getting promoted to the twelfth grade next year, and I'm worried about going to 12-A next year and that's about all. That's for the kids that do good. I think I'll probably drop down to 12-B. I like the kids in A-section better. Kids in B-section always fussing. See, like if you make an A in history or answer more questions, they're gon get mad because you're Miss Know-It-All.

•　　•　　•

The best thing that ever happened to me, I guess, is when I got promoted to 11-A. Because when I was in the ninth grade I was pretty dumb — I thought. And when I was in the tenth grade I was okay because I made A's and B's, then when I went to 11-A I know it was something big because I hadn't been in A-section since I left elementary school. A-section supposed to be the smartest section at school.

— Do you worry a lot about your grades?

Yeah. Yeah, all the time. I just worry about them all the time. And, I don't know, I feel like getting Miss Ragsdale and throwing her outdoors, that's about all. Because she gave me an F this six weeks. She's my English and Spanish teacher. I always get a headache every day when I go to her class. She picks on the kids that sit on the back rows where I sit. The kids on the first row always get A's and B's, and the ones on the back always get D's and F's. It don't matter whether they got their work or not.

— Do you expect to finish school?

Yes. Definitely.

— Why do you want to finish?

I just want to go ahead and finish and get out on my own. I just want to leave home, and I'll leave the same day I finish school. I'll pack my bags the day before.

— So where will you go?

My brother in New York gon send me to trade school or college. My sister told me he would send me.

Yeah, I want to go to college because, Miss Lofton, my history teacher, said she had a lot of fun, so I would like to have some fun too. And I just want to go so I can further my education, to learn that much more about life and school and everything. And if you don't have an education, then the jobs that you want, you probably can't get it or something like that.

．　　．　　．

I'm the most nervous, I guess, when I have to go up on the stage. Like at school, we have to say our prayers in Spanish, and I still haven't learned it. When we had graduation from elementary school, boy, I was really nervous then. Or either when I have to make a report in class. I'm not used to getting up in front of all those kids and they just be looking dead at me, and most of 'em — yeah, all of 'em — they want to hear what I have to say because they always think I have something stupid to say.

．　　．　　．

— What's the greatest thing wrong with your school?

We don't have anything for the boys to do. While we out for summer break they don't have anything to do at school like they do at other schools. You know, at other schools they have track, baseball diamonds, football fields — we don't have any of that at our school. Any time during the year. There isn't no football team or baseball team at our school.

— Does the white high school here have a baseball and football field?

Yeah.

— How do you explain that?

Well, I don't know. Because ever since I know, they had one and we didn't.

— How many white teachers are there at your school?

One. I had her in the tenth grade. She was nice and she was fair.

— Do you think your school should have more white teachers?

Well, no. They don't have any colored over to Hampton County High, the white school.

— Do you think there should be more colored teachers at the white school and more white teachers at the colored school?

No, I just think it should be all white at Hampton County High and all colored over here. Because, you know, when the colored teachers get around the white students they're gon give the white students better grades than they do the colored students even though they try. There aren't any white students at our school either. There are about forty colored at the white school.

— Would you like there to be white students at your school?

Well, if there was colored at theirs, I would. I think they should be even. If colored go over there, the same number of whites should come over here.

— Do you think the schools should be completely integrated?

No, I don't think we should be at all. I just don't wanna be mixed with the white. I just been with the colored all my life; still have to be with 'em without being mixed up.

But next year we're gon be integrated. And by the way those kids talk — the colored ones — we gon have some trouble. And I don't wanna be there. Like Joe always telling us about what he gon do to those girls, those white girls. He told me that he gon get one every day and make her have a baby, and then he know their mama ain't gon make *him* marry her. And Jerry talk about he going to bring guns every day with him, which he sometime do now.

·　　·　　·

Oh, guess what? We gon get our senior class rings this spring instead of next year. My math teacher said we gon get 'em now so the white students won't get up there and try to change things, try to make the rings be like theirs. So there won't be no Rebel on the rings. We got Tigers, they got Rebels.

·　　·　　·

— How often is the racial issue discussed in your school?

Mostly every Tuesday, Wednesday, and Friday, when we go to math. The teacher, he talk about mostly what we don't have and what they do have, and what we will get when we do integrate schools and everything. He said we might get a track field then because they have one and they be wanting one and they'd go to the principal and he'd probably try to get it. He be talking about they have fans in the summertime and we don't and they got air conditioning in some of the rooms and we don't have any.

And Miss Lofton, my history teacher, she used to talk about it all the time, but she don't that much now.

I'm Somebody Important

— What are some things she talked about?

Well, I don't know really, because I always be keeping up a lot of fuss, we be singing and doing some of everything. She was talking about how they treated the black people — I don't know really. She said the white always had the black behind them ever since she know, and that every time the black try to get ahead the white always push him further back down.

— Do you agree with that?

Some of the time, some of the time I don't. See, some things I agree with and some I don't. Like one I don't, she think the school should be integrated, I think, and I don't. And I forget what else she talk about. I don't know. I don't try to keep up with all that.

— Do other history teachers discuss race?

Most history teachers, they never even thought about the subject. None of the teachers except my math teacher and Miss Lofton talk about it.

— Do you think they should?

No, I think they should stay on their subject they supposed to be teaching. Because I find that the ones that don't talk about it are more interesting than the ones that do. Because the ones that don't, I can get a lesson more better. And the ones that do, like they be talking about one subject one minute and the next be talking about white and black, and I get all confused.

— Do you like the way Miss Lofton teaches now or the way she taught when she was talking about race all the time?

The way she teaches now. I can get my lesson better now than when she be skipping from this to that. Then I wasn't paying any attention because I wasn't interested, and now I am. Now we're learning about the presidency and slavery — did they want slavery abolished or slavery and all that.

— That's racial, isn't it?

Yeah, I know, but it's not like the way she used to talk about it.

•　　•　　•

When I was in about the first or second grade my mother say I couldn't go in the drugstore and sit down. One day my sister and me was going uptown and I told my sister, "I bet I take a seat in there and sit down and rest," because everywhere I used to go I used to sit down because I was tired. My sister told my mama, and then my mama told me I'm not supposed to sit down in there. I told her white people sit down there, said how come I couldn't, and she just told me to get out of the house. So I told her a thousand times, I believe, that I wouldn't sit in them, but she still wouldn't let me go uptown.

Janice Riley

— Did you ever have any white playmates?

Yeah, one. Jim Johnson's daughter, her father owns all the peanut things, you know. My mama was working for 'em all the time when I was about four, and she'd take me to their house just about every day and we'd play together. She was real nice and she still is, but they sending her to a private school. They don't want her to be around colored people and I sure don't wanna be around her.

— Do you ever see her now?

Yeah, I see her every day now. She be getting off the bus when I be coming home from the post office — the bus that take her to the private school and back. No, we don't talk. She always wave or something.

— Why do you think you are not still good friends?

I don't know, I think we still is. I don't really know.

• • •

— Have you ever wished you were someone else?

Once. I wish I was white when I was small, but not anymore. When I was six or seven I thought about that all the time. I wished I was white because I wouldn't have gotten so many whippings then. Because I don't care how bad the white kids be, their mama don't never even whip 'em. At least I never seen any of 'em whip 'em. She always smile at 'em or something like that.

— When did you stop wishing you were white?

Well, when I was in the sixth grade. I started hating 'em then.

— What happened to make you start hating them?

I don't know, I just hate 'em. I don't hate 'em and I don't like 'em, I don't know.

— But what happened in the sixth grade?

Well, let me see, I don't know.

— Nothing specific happened to bring about this change?

Let me think. Well, one thing this drugstore man — he used to hate black peoples — and he burnt up a couple of colored people's houses. He said that all niggers ought to be in a place locked up, that they ain't got sense enough to be around here and like that. And I hated him, so I started hating every white person I met, I guess, I don't know. I don't hate 'em and I don't like 'em and I don't love 'em. That's it.

— Have you ever hit a white person?

I hit a little boy, he called me a nigger. Boy, that's been a long time, that was '67. I was with Sally, we was taking out some invitations for her sister because she was finishing school that year. And a little white boy went by on his bicycle and he called me a nigger and then he throwed a rock at me. And I just walked up there and knocked him off the bicycle and told him to go tell his mama.

— How do you feel when you hear someone say *nigger*?

I feel like knocking their head off.

— Why do you think it is that you don't like white people now?

Well, I don't know, I heard so much about 'em till I just hate 'em. I don't hate nobody, I just don't like 'em. I've heard so much from people talking. Like Miss Lofton and some of the other teachers at school and just my mama some-time. The teachers say white people have their way all their life — that what Miss Lofton say — and every time we try to get up, they push us down or something.

And my mama was up at where she worked at, and this white lady called Sarah said she done got her kids and send them to a private school and she was glad her kids didn't have to be mixed up in all that. And my mother told her that when the white kids was small, they wanted colored people to raise 'em, but now since they got up some size, they don't want us around 'em. See, my mother used to take care of some little white kids. And they just got to arguing, but most parents won't stand up to white people.

— Are there any white people that you do like?

No. I don't like them in a way and in a way I do. Some of 'em nice in a way and some of 'em ain't in a way. Jim Johnson's daughter's okay.

— Do you think most whites look at blacks as full and equal human beings?

I don't know, I don't think so. I don't think they look at us as equals, because we're not. We're not equal in nothing. Most of them have more money and most of them can get probably most anything they want because they're white. You know, like a white boy and a colored boy go for the same job, the white boy mostly get it.

— Do you think there are many white people who are prejudiced?

Well, I don't know. Let me see — some of them, I do believe. Like this lady that live way up going to the post office. She jealous, that's one thing I know. She jealous of this colored preacher down here, Reverend Bishop. One time I heard her talking to the man that live next door to her, and she said she don't think Reverend Bishop should be in that fine a house and everything, down here. She just said she don't know but one nigger that live in that fine a house and she don't think he deserves it.

— Why do you think whites think they're better than blacks?

I guess because they had their way all their life . . . They just know it, I guess, they don't think it. I don't know why they think it; I guess because — I don't know!

— How do you feel about racial discrimination?

In a way I don't like it. Because the whites — boy! — they get next to me. I just don't like 'em, just don't like their looks at times.

— What's the best way to behave around white people?

Not to even see 'em, I guess. You see 'em and you don't see 'em. See, like I see you, but I don't want to pay you no attention so I don't see you.

— How do most blacks act around whites?

Most of the older menfolk, they like 'em, I think. They always run up in their face, trying to talk to 'em or something. You know, they always patting 'em on the shoulder, tell 'em they know 'em when they was small and all that. And I don't like it.

— Do young people act differently?

Yeah. I don't never see any of them run up to their face and always trying to talk to 'em or something like that. Because if he did, the other guys would talk about him, so he won't do it no more. See, they'll just kind of talk about you to your face and then you'll get ashamed and won't do it no more.

— Tell me about some white people you know.

Most of the white people I know are the people who run the stores and Jim Johnson, most of his people. Miss Chester, she own the store up there where I get most of my things from, shoes and pants. She's a sometimes person. Mostly when my mother be around she's nice. But when she's not around, she's like some old mean white lady. She just sit around and look at you and turn up her nose.

And this other guy at the post office, we always get into it about stamps and saying *yes sir*. He always telling me to say *yes sir* to him, and "Don't throw the money down on the counter." Like when I give him six cents for a stamp, I put it in his hand. But when he give me the stamp, he just throw it on the counter and walk on. And then when I do his money like that, he get mad with me. He tells me his hand was out there and I could of put it there. I tell him my hand was out there and he could of put the stamp in it, and I wasn't gon say *yes sir,* I was gon say *yes.* He don't say nothing. Most of the time I just get my stamp and walk out. Sometimes I don't get it and ask for my six cents back. Then I don't mail the letter. And then when I go in there again, he don't wait on me, he send somebody else.

— Do you try to keep from having anything to do with white people?

Yeah. Like I meet some on the streets and they ask me some question, I tell 'em I don't know. Like they say, "Where Century Village?" I tell 'em, "Look around, see for yourself," or "I don't know." I tell 'em some stupid thing. And

when we at school and some old white man want to find some information — where the principal's office at — he don't know where it at. We don't know either.

And I like to run into white people a lot. Like they walking down the street not paying no attention, I just like to bump into 'em and nearly knock 'em down. Me and Gwen do that all the time. We just say, "Watch this," and we just run into 'em.

— What do you think about white people calling black people by their first names even when they might be older?

Well, I don't like it because if I was older and go in a white man's house and call their wife by their first name, they would get mad and probably kick me out. And I just don't like it because if one come here asking me where is Margaret — that's my grandmother — I don't know Margaret unless she come to the door. I tell them Mrs. Campbell or Mrs. Margaret Campbell live here but don't no Margaret or Margaret Campbell live here.

— How many white people have you told that to?

I told one, the insurance man. I hate him. He so fresh! He's always talking to me about my boyfriends, then he'll wink his eye at me and everything, and I just don't like him. I told him he better go find another woman to wink his eye at, because I'm not one of them.

— You told him that?

Yeah, that what I felt like telling him. And then one day I'm walking down the road and he was coming up the road and his car splashed some water on me and I told him I was gon get some and throw it back on him. But my grandmama told me if I do, she gon beat me, so I didn't.

— Does your grandmother say *yes sir* and *no sir* to white people?

Yeah, but I don't think she should. I tell her that all the time when she start fussing at me about not saying *sir,* and then I leave before she start again. Like they call here for her on the phone and they say "Margaret home?" I say "yeah" or something like that. Then she get mad when she hang up and she start fussing at me. She tell me that if *she* can say *yes sir* and *no sir,* I can too. I told her I wasn't fixing to say that. She told me she say it, she think I should. And she get to fussing and I just can't stand it.

•　　•　　•

— How do you feel about some white people having a lot of money while almost no black people do?

Well, I think they deserve it in most cases because their father left them his farm, and mine didn't. So they probably deserved it and I didn't.

— How do you feel about Jim Johnson having so much money?

Well, in a way I like it, and in a way I don't. It's okay because his fathers and people, they was able to give it to him, so I guess it should be. But most of it be made by colored people working, slavery — it was a long time ago — used to have to work and not get paid that much money.

— Is it still that way?

No, I don't think so.

• • •

— What changes would you like to see in relations between blacks and whites?

I wanna see 'em get along more better and that's about all.

— Do you think that will ever happen?

Nope. I don't think so.

— Do you think the racial situation has gotten any better in the last five years?

Gotten better? Gotten worse to me. In what way I don't know. Because at first when they started protesting, they wanted to be *with* the white. But now they protesting that they don't wanna be with the white or something like that, I don't know. It got me confused.

— Which do you agree with, protesting to be with the whites or not to be with whites?

Not to be with 'em. I don't see why they wanna be with 'em. I don't feel that we should be integrated. Schools and everything else. Maybe the restaurants and things like that should, but not the schools. The churches shouldn't be, they should be having their own private meetings.

— What about housing?

Well, I don't know, because most Negroes, boy, they don't have no sense. They always mess up or tear up or something, so I think it should be just like it is now.

— You mean remain poor and keep living in bad houses?

Not poor, but not all mixed up with the whites because I don't wanna be around 'em that much. I guess I get enough of looking at 'em every day already. I get tired of looking at 'em. Every time I go up the streets I see about a thousand different white people.

— What's most important to you: being shown respect, integration, or equal job opportunities?

I can pick two? Respect and having equal job opportunities. The most important is having equal job opportunities and making more money.

— Do you wish the racial situation was such so that you and Jim Johnson's daughter could still be friends?

No. I just don't want no white persons as my friend. I just hate 'em, now. No, I never hated nobody. But I hate 'em now.

— What happened to make you change your mind?

They had a meeting at school the other day and I couldn't go in it. There were some white students from Hampton County High and their principal and some students from our school talking about integration next year, and I wanted to be in it, and they wouldn't let me. Mr. Franklin, the white principal, he wouldn't let me in when I asked to get in. I wanted to be one of the delegates but they wouldn't let me.

— Is God white or black?

He black. Yeah, in my opinion, He's black. Every picture I see that pretend it's God, it's white. So I say my God is black and let theirs be white and that's that.

•   •   •

— What do you think white people worry about most?

The black folks trying to take over. They worry about that because they don't wanna be under the blacks saying *yes sir* and *no sir* — to them.

Well, I don't know what I would think of that situation. I think most blacks would be like most white is now. They would try to take it all for theirself, and, you know, not care about nobody else.

— How do whites keep the power?

I guess by their friends voting for 'em and everything. And most blacks, I don't care if it was one of their best friends running for something, they not gon vote for him, they gon vote for the white man. Makes me sick. They say Mister Whatever-white-man-running gon give them what they want and when the black man get up there he ain't gon do nothing, and how they know I don't know! That's the way it was in Hendersonville. Rev. Burton, he was running for something, and it's three times more blacks in Hendersonville than it is white and Rev. Burton could have got it if they had all voted for him. But they didn't, they went and voted for some white man. I think Rev. Burton got twenty votes out of all the peoples in Hendersonville.

— If a black and a white were running for mayor, which one would you vote for?

The black one. I don't care how bad he was, I vote for him still. I just wanna see one black person in power. I just wanna see *one* black person beating a white person in something.

.   .   .

— Do you think black people ever attempt to keep other black people down?

Yeah, those ones that is prejudiced against other black people. They just think they're gon get more than they're gon get or they got more than they got or something like that. They just have mostly what they want. I know some like that. It's some that live across from my mother and, boy, you get anything more than what they got, they gon get mad with you. Probably won't speak to you until they get something like it that cost more or something like that. Like one time my mother bought a record player and the people across the street had to go get them one.

.   .   .

— Pretend I'm your kid and tell me about race.

Oh, I don't know what I would say, because I ain't even planning on having no kids.

— You told me the other day you wanted six kids.

Not no more. I don't know why I changed my mind. I don't know, I don't know what I want to do. I ain't gon have no kids, huh-uh, they're too worrisome.

— Do you still want to get married?

No. I just don't wanna marry. I plan to go in the Army now. I made up my mind today. And a Army WAC, she ain't supposed to be married. Made up my mind when I went with a friend to see the counselor, and when she went in there to see the counselor, I just picked up a book on the Army.

— What's Wally going to think?

I don't know. I probably gon be changed my mind by tonight or tomorrow. I change my mind every day. I have a different idea every day, I guess.

·　　·　　·

— Do you believe anyone powerful cares about the condition poor people are in?

I don't know, but I don't think so. Like Nixon, he say he was gon give 'em more money on their checks and things, so they can have people tear down these old houses and build new ones, and he never did nothing. He said that when he ran for president so people would vote for him.

— What did you think about President Kennedy?

Well, I liked him in a way and in a way I didn't. Some things that he said he was gon do, he did it.

— You said in a way you didn't like him . . .

Because he was white.

— What famous black leader do you respect most?

Reverend Ralph David Abernathy. I even talked to him one day on the telephone. We called him at school in Miss Lofton's class. I didn't have no question to ask him so my friend gave me a question. And then I called him again when I got home from school, but I couldn't get him. I don't know what I was gon talk to him about, I was gon think of something. I asked the operator for the number of the Southern Christian Leadership something and she gave it to me. When they answered they said he was out. They said, "You wanna leave him a message?" I said, "No, that's okay."

— Have you ever heard of the NAACP or the Black Panthers?

I never heard of the first one you said, but I've heard of the Black Panthers.

— What do you think about blacks who say you need to use violence to bring about change?

What do I think about it? Well, I wouldn't mind doing it. For me, it would be a good thing, because I wouldn't mind beating up on a couple of people's heads.

— Whose?

A whole lot of white ones. Not all of 'em. The ones that was fighting back, I guess.

• • •

— Do you like the country or the city better?

The country probably, because I can do more here than I can in the city. Like walk the streets when I get ready. But I probably walk the streets up there at twelve or one o'clock — which I don't do down here, somebody steal me or kidnap me or something. And you can grow more here than you can there. In some ways I like the city better and in some ways I don't.

— What are some of the ways you like it better?

Well, it's big and you have a lot of places to go.

— What are the ways you don't like it?

Well, to me, there aren't that many boys, you can't meet that many friends in a big place. I didn't when I was there.

I like the country and probably will be living in it. Because that's all Wally talk about. He says there's more grass and he can plant a garden or something.

• • •

— Do you go to church?

Yeah, every Sunday just about.

— How do you feel in church?

All right. Just that I don't like to usher. I don't like to stand up and people be watching you, see what you gon do, see if you gon make a mistake or something. I don't like it. I have to usher on the second Sunday of every two months mostly. See, like when the preacher stand up to open the door to the church, you suppose to take some chairs up to the front if there be children to sit in them that will join the church, and most of the time we always mess up. We take it at the wrong time or something like that. And everybody be watching.

• • •

— Do you think God punishes people for sins they commit?

Yeah, but who I don't know.

— Have you ever been punished for your sins?

Huh-uh, I don't know of any bad ones I did yet. I said yet because —
nothing. It's nothing. I want to burn up somebody — a used-to-be-friend, Bessie.
She's a little old girl in the seventh grade. She's always running up to my face
telling me something about Sally and J.B. — he's supposed to be Sally's boyfriend — and telling me how I'm always trying to take somebody's boyfriend
and she and Sally are gon get me. And I just feel like just striking a match and
burning her up. One day I'm gon do it. Yeah, I'm serious. I'm gon burn her;
if I don't burn her all the way up, I'm gon burn her half way. Boy, she get
next to me.

· · ·

— If you died, would you like to come back as a haint?

Uh-huh! I think about that. I just tell my little sister all the time if I die
before she do I'm gon pull her hair every night. Boy, I'd haint everybody that
I . . . Especially Wally. I just want to figure out what he be doing; if he be
doing anything wrong, I'd get him.

· · ·

What I'm most afraid of besides haints? Only thing — seeing somebody
get kilt. I ain't never seen it, but if I do I probably be dead myself. I just
scared. I just don't wanna see all that blood. I think about that all the time.
I think about somebody having nerve enough to cut somebody or shoot 'em and
all that. I wouldn't wanna be around 'em when they dead, they probably kill me.

— Have you ever thought about killing anyone?

Yeah, everybody I see mostly. Mostly it's my little sister, I feel like killing
her every day. Feel like it at least.

— Have you ever seriously thought about killing someone?

No, just myself. Last time I thought about it was Saturday night, because
I couldn't go uptown. See, now they so stupid that the colored policeman, he
don't want no young teen-agers at the café unless their mother be with 'em.
And I just wanted to go and I couldn't and I got mad. I told Becky, my sister,
I was gon kill myself, and she just followed me all around like I was gon do
it for real.

Yeah, I thought seriously about doing it. See, we have a icepick and I
picked it up . . . I wasn't gon do it, I don't think, I don't know . . . I don't know
what was going across my mind. My sister snatched it out my hand like she was
crazy or something, she thought I was gon do it. I don't know if I would have.
I had that much nerve Saturday night but I don't know.

I'm Somebody Important

— Before the other night, had you ever picked up an icepick and thought about stabbing yourself with it?

Just held it up? Yeah, I go in the kitchen and get 'em all the time, thinking about killing myself or something, but I don't get the nerve enough to stick myself with it. And sometimes I thought about going outside, getting the ax, cutting my head off, but huh-uh. And then I felt like shooting myself. And I still don't believe I'd die if I did, because I wouldn't know the right place to shoot. See, I wanna die just like that. I don't even want to remember nothing. Just die! I don't wanna have no pains or nothing.

— What are some other times you thought about killing yourself?

Well, I thought about it when Wally left after he came down here the other day and . . . Lemme see, some other times . . . I can't remember.

— What about in the past?

I haven't been thinking about it then, I just be thinking about running away then. And now if I kill myself, it'll be that much better. Then I won't have to live no more and I just be dead and everybody be crying and feeling sorry for me then. But if I just run away, they probably just come get me.

— Do you think you will ever really kill yourself?

I don't know. I might; knowing me, I might.

— Have you ever thought it would be a bad thing to die?

No, not yet. I don't think it will.

— Do you think you'd go to heaven?

I don't know. My grandmother told me I ain't. She tell me that all the time when I say I'm gon kill myself. She said I wasn't going because I been too bad.

•   •   •

— What person that you know do you admire most?

I guess it's Elizabeth, a girl in 12-A. She's real smart and everything, everybody like her, she's real nice. I like the way she act toward people. She real nice.

— Are you nice?

Compared to Elizabeth, no.

— Do you think it's good to be nice?

Yeah, you have more friends that way. I have only one girlfriend. The rest of 'em, everybody hate me, except the guys. Every guy in Bradford my friend. People tell me I'm more popular with the boys than I is with the girls.

•   •   •

— What would be one thing you would change about the world if you could?

The president. I just wanna see a black president. I don't know why, I guess I just wanna see a black man, see what he can do.

. . .

Right now I'm making my vegetable garden. I ain't put nothing in it. I have a garden because I just want to be doing something.

— Are you pretty good at growing vegetables?

Huh-uh. Because when I planted my garden the other year, I planted some peas, some corn, collards, and some okra, and I didn't have but one pea come up.

. . .

— Suppose you could be born as somebody else — who would you want to be?

The president's daughter.

— How come?

I don't know, I just want to be somebody important. I just want to be important for once.

— What do you mean by important?

Well, like somebody that got a responsibility or something like that, just being nice and everything.

Sammy Jackson

Sammy Jackson lives alone with his father on a backwoods dirt road about five miles from Shady Grove, Georgia. Their nearest neighbors are a mile away. Sammy has that manner of nonchalance that many sixteen-year-olds take on. He moves leisurely and speaks in a drawl. During the interviews he never raised his voice in excitement or anger.

My mama died when I was five years old. I don't know how she died, she just got sick and died. She just died overnight at home. I was here, but I didn't know she was dying, but I knew it the next morning. My father saw that she was dead, and he just woke up me and my older brother and told us she was dead. It was four of us then, but my little brother and sister was kind of small so he didn't bother too much about telling them. Then he went around and told everybody and then he called the ambulance and they come and got her.

— How did you feel when she died?

Well, really, I didn't feel too strange, I didn't feel so bad about it, because I was so small that I didn't really understand nothing about . . . you know, death.

— What did your brothers and sister do after she died?

After my mother died, one of my aunts that stay in New York, she took my sister. And one of my uncles stay up in Charlestown, this town about ten miles from here, he took my baby brother. So just me and my older brother stayed here after my mother died. See, he was about seven and I was about five. We was the biggest two, so we just stayed on with Daddy. See, the other two was real young and they needed more of a mother than me and my older brother did, so that's why those two was taken out.

Daddy wanted us to stay here and keep him company, you know, so he wouldn't just be here by himself. Another reason, you know, was for us to help around the house and work around the house and stuff like that.

My older brother ain't here now, because he went into the Jobs Corps last year. See, he was going to school and his books . . . He wasn't real smart, you know, he just didn't care nothing about the books. I mean he just couldn't help it, it just wasn't in him to learn. But otherwise he was real smart; he could fix mostly anything. And he failed a couple of grades, so he just quit school. And he heard about the Job Corps and he decided he would go in and take him up a trade. He's taking up auto mechanics.

— Do you remember anything about your mother?

Well, one thing about her, she was kind of strict on the things that me and Junior did. Like when we was going to school we used to shoot marbles. And we shoot marbles, we get down on our knees and get our clothes all nasty. Most of the time we tear them on the knee. And she was real strict about that. She didn't want us to do it and if we did do it and come back home with pants tore, she would whip us.

First good whipping I remember is when I was small. It used to be a big bush that set right over there, it was one of her favorite flowers. We had a old tricycle Junior got for Christmas, so I used to call that my trike. And so I get over there in the flower and ride through it and break it down, and she told me not to do it. But I just kept on doing it. She grabbed me off and throwed me down and whipped me, and my nose started bleeding and everything. I mean, I don't guess she meant to throw me down. You know, she was so big and I was small, she just knocked me down when she grabbed me.

•　　•　　•

— How have you gotten along with your father through the years?

I say I get along with him okay, everything all right. Sometime, you know, I might not like the things he do. I disagree with him sometime but nothing really serious about it.

— What are some things he does that you don't like?

I say like Sunday we was going to church in the car and the aerial broke off and he turned on the radio anyway. And I told him it wouldn't play like that without an aerial. And he said it would and he just cut it on and just kept up a whole bunch of noise. He tried to find different stations, but he wouldn't never get it to play. So finally he cut it off; it made me real mad about it. It seemed to me that common sense would have told him that it wouldn't play without an aerial.

— Do you remember the maddest you ever got at your father?

I would say one of the maddest times was last year about November; he being real strict on when for me to come in. I think it was about 12:30 that night when I come in. You know, he usually want me to come in before 12, about 11:30 or something like that. It was about 12:30 when I come that night, so he was laying up. He had a little switch when I walked in the door, and he drawed back to hit me and I wouldn't let him whip me. And he talked a whole bunch of trash and bunch of junk, just talking about fooling around with the wrong crowd and disobedient children don't live all their days and stuff like that, and I went into the kitchen and got me a knife. And I got into bed, he just kept on talking and I talking back at him. I was mad. I mean, if Daddy hit me I don't know what I would of did; I might would of cut him or killed him, I don't know.

— What are some good things about your father?

Well, I'll say mostly — not everything — but I say most any small thing I want, I mostly get it. Like if I want some money and don't have any, he'll give me some. And I ask him to let me use the car, get somebody else to drive for me, he'll let me have it, so far.

— What are some bad points?

Some of the bad points that I see is him fussing all the time, being so strict. I mean, he ain't exactly strict, but if I just be a few minutes late, he just fussing and going on. And he don't want me to drink. He just fuss at me, just tells me I'll catch up with myself after a while about being hard-headed. And, you know, I just hate for him to fuss at me. I would rather for him to whip me than go on and fuss.

— What rules has your father set down for you?

Well, I don't exactly have any rules, but it's some things he tell me that I shouldn't do. That's sassing grown folks, talking back to 'em and stuff like that. And that I should go to church every Sunday.

— What is the main difference between your youth and your father's?

Well, we have more modern things now than they had back in his day. I mean, we have TV's. You mean my life or just any average children? [Sammy doesn't have a TV.]

— Both.

And we have TV's and radios and different things now. He said when they was small, heck, they couldn't go out; if he went anywhere he had to be back before sundown, before the sun go down. And he couldn't ever go out till he was about grown. And me, you know, at least I started off when I was about fourteen; I didn't exactly have a girlfriend that I went to see then, but I would go out around the crossroads to the juke up there. That's about it.

— Do you think your father would like you to be the way he was?

Well, it seem to me that's the way he would want it. I mean he said he don't mind me going out and going to see a girl, but I don't know. It seem like that though by the way he talk all the time — say that's the way his mother and father used to treat him, that they would have to be in before sundown, and he talk about how we just getting badder than children was in his day and all that.

— Do you wish your mother were still living?

Yes.

— Why?

I don't know. I couldn't answer that, I just wish she was living.

— What has it been like growing up without a mother?

Well, I mean, seem like that we did a mother's job, a wife's job, like cooking and stuff like that, cleaning up, sweeping the yard, make up the beds, feed chickens, and stuff like that. See, I cook supper every night, cook cornbread or some peas or something like that, cook fatback during the week and on weekends maybe pork chops or chicken.

And I don't know, I would say that boys always like their mothers best and girls always like their fathers best. I will just say motherly love, I didn't get that. And I believe I would be different if she was living.

— In what ways?

I don't know. I guess I'd be different ... I mean, staying out late, that would be one thing; I'd come in on time, stuff like that.

•　　•　　•

The first time I started school I was only five years old — I was too young really, and so after about five months I stopped and waited to the next year. Anyway, the first day of school I had on these shoes that come up about as high as boots, string them up. Had a pair of overall pants, had on an old shirt, had me an old iron pipe. It wasn't really a pipe that smoked, it had a piece of wire made in the shape of a pipe, had it sticking in my pocket. So I went to school. I was kind of scared, but not too scared. But when I was small I was shamefaced and I wouldn't talk much; all when I was little I was like that. So I had to go to the bathroom and I wouldn't ask the teacher and I went in my clothes and they had

to take my clothes off and clean them. Put on a big old robe, I walked around in that for the rest of the school day.

•   •   •

I been going to the white school for about four years. I started in the seventh grade and next year I'll be in the eleventh. Reason I decided to transfer, I just got to where I didn't like the teachers at the black school, the way they act, so I just figured if I go down there to the white school I would have it better. See, one thing, in the black school if you didn't get up your homework and things like that, they'll whip you next day. I didn't get too many whippings then, but just the way they treat some of the other children, I just didn't like that. It made me feel just as though I was getting a whipping myself. I did get two or three, but I don't think any of 'em were because I didn't get up my lessons. I was real smart then. I got up all my lessons, I didn't make nothing but A's and B's; real smart. But the whipping, that's the main reason I went to the white school.

After they had the freedom-of-choice plan, I just wanted to go and give it a try, you know, to see whether it was better. The first year it came out, I started to go but I didn't have enough courage. There wasn't no other black student to go that year. But the next year I went and there was about fifteen of us and about three or four hundred white students.

— Why did you think the white school might be better?

Well, I figured since they was white that there wouldn't be any of this whipping going on, that the parents wouldn't approve of the children being whipped like that. I figured that a black parent just wouldn't care; they'll just say the children probably needed the whipping and that maybe it'll make 'em do better the next time. But I don't believe a white parent would want everybody whipping on their child.

— Tell me about your first day in the white school.

Well, the first day at the white school I was kind of ... I wasn't exactly scared but I was excited, being my first day. It was a whole lot different. I mean, I didn't know nobody, didn't know nothing about the building. It was just ... I don't know, I can't describe it. I mean, going to school at Marshall — that's the black school — when I started off the first day there, my brother and all my cousins and things was there, and it just kind of made me feel good. But at the white school, you had some black students but it was more white than it was black and it was just a lot different.

— Did any of the white students come up to you and talk to you the first day?

Right. It wasn't too many, mostly boys, but it was enough to make you feel like you was wanted. They just asked a whole bunch of questions, showed me around the schoolhouse, told me teachers' names, and things like that.

— How did you like the school after you had been going there for a while?

Well, I liked it real good. When I started, I just had it in mind just to go about three years, just up to the tenth grade, and then go back to Marshall; after around the tenth, they don't hardly whip you too much there. So I was planning on going back, but after I got down there, I come to like it, so I just stayed on down there.

— Why do you like it better?

Just everything a whole lot better — the children, the teachers, and I like the school.

— The children at the white school are better?

Right. It's just the way they treats you. I mean they just treats you good.

— The children at the black school don't treat you good?

I mean they treat you all right, but the white children, they just different.

— Describe the difference.

I know the difference, but I just can't describe it. You know, I just can't put it in words. It just seems like they treat you better. I mean, in a way they make you feel like you're wanted and everything, and make you feel like you're needed. But when you going to Marshall, it just seem like that you just going there because that was the only school you could go to.

— When you first started going to the white school, did any of the students call you a nigger?

About the first two years I never did have no trouble like that. But about the third year, after they find me out real good, some of 'em called me a nigger then.

Sometime we be sitting up in the room, say just discussing social studies or something like that, and they'll say, "Well, this weekend I heard about a nigger man got killed," or something like that. Well, they're sitting up in the class like that in front of everybody and it makes me mad, but I don't say anything. But like if we just be standing around talking and one just call me a nigger, that burns me up sometime.

Like one day we was in agricultural class, and I was standing around in the door. A boy walked by there. He said, "Move out of the way, nigger." I said, "What'd you say?" He said, "You heard me, nigger." We had a fight, and then some more boys, they told us we better cool it before the teacher walked in and catch us.

Sammy Jackson 133

— So it burns you up when you hear the word *nigger?*

Well, it's just according to what mood I be in. Sometimes it makes me mad and sometimes I don't care. I mean, if I be mad, if I just be mad with anybody, it just burns me up. But like if I'm just talking and they just say, "I know a nigger that lives somewhere," or something or other like that, it don't bother me.

— Do you believe that most of the white students aren't or are prejudiced?

I'd say most of 'em aren't, because we never had any trouble, I mean any racial difference.

— How many use the word *nigger?*

I wouldn't say all of 'em, I wouldn't even say 50 percent.

— Do you believe there is any difference between white people in high school and their parents?

I'll say there's a lot of difference between the students now and the parents. I would say that an older person wouldn't care too much for the black because their parents brought them up to hate 'em, not to associate with 'em. But now everybody going together, schools going together and all that bit, it really doesn't make any difference with 'em now.

— Do you have any real good friends who are white?

Right.

— How many?

I'll say most of 'em at school. And I have some friends that are better than others, that are closer, but all of 'em are nice and everything.

— Do you have any white friends you do anything with outside of school?

I mean, I've been invited to several parties and things, but I never did go.

— Why?

Because of the parents, you know what I mean. It might not make any difference with the white students, but being black, the parents might not want me, you know, want me in the house. And another thing, us being black going to their party might make them lose some of their friends, white friends.

— Do you have any real close white friends you hang around with after school?

I have about one real close; I mean not real close, but I mean I consider him as close, being real nice.

— What do you do together?

I mean, we don't really do anything together; we just hang around together at the schoolhouse, talk all the time, might ride downtown or something like that.

•   •   •

— How many black students go to the white school now?

About twenty-five.

— How do you feel about being one of the few black young people that went to the white school?

Well, to tell you the truth, really, I'm glad that I'm one of the first ones that went, because it looks like the first ones that went had a better time than some of the ones that came down later. I mean, look like they just treat us better or something, we get along with them, the white students, better than the ones that came down there later. So I would say that I feel kind of good about it.

And I would say that most of the boys that came down later, that didn't go the first year, most of them were scared to go down and their parents scared for 'em to go down there. And after they saw that we didn't have no trouble down there, they just come on. And it just let everybody see that we wasn't really scared, I would say. But next year the schools are coming together, and everybody will be going to the same school.

— What do your black friends who still go to the black school think of you going to the white school?

Well, most of 'em like it, because most of 'em want to go. I mean they looking forward for next year, all of us going together. Most of 'em seem like they're glad of it.

— What do the white students think of the schools coming together?

Well, we talked about it one day. How it would be, both schools just becoming one school. We talked about what it would be like, would the different children coming in affect our class, what the different changes be made. Most of 'em I talked to didn't mind, but a few of 'em, I would say they didn't like the idea so good. They said that the classes would be too large and they just wouldn't learn as much as they would with the classes being small as they is now.

— Are you in favor of the schools coming together?

It don't make any difference to me.

— Which one do you lean toward?

It don't make any difference with me. I mean, since they had the freedom-of-choice plan, everybody was going where they wanted. It suited me fine like that.

— Which way would you seriously prefer — for the schools to stay separate or to come together?

Well, to tell you the truth, I would rather for it to stay like it is, separate. Because some of the children, the black children, bunch of 'em talking about how they gon do next year, how they gon whip one every day, whip a white student every day, and all kind of stuff like that. And I mean by us just having such a peaceful time with 'em, I just wouldn't want 'em just to be starting at 'em. The white students could have had us in the same situation when we first went down there, all of 'em could have just jumped on us, just have a whole big mess.

• • •

— Do you like school?

No. I just don't like it. It's just going to school studying, I just don't like studying, stuff like that. I just don't like it.

— What kind of grades do you make?

I'll say I'm about a C+ student. I could be an A student but I don't study like I used to. I mean I study just enough to pass, but I used to study and I was real smart, and I could be an A now.

— Why did you come down?

Well, after I started going out, you know, I just started caring less about it.

— Have you ever thought of dropping out?

No. Without an education, you might as well be dead. I mean in this day and time you just can't make it without education. I mean it have been time when it didn't matter whether you had education or not. But now most jobs you get require college education.

— Do you plan on going to college?

Huh-uh. Since I hate school so bad I just don't see any way possible I go to college. I mean, I'll probably go, but it won't be right after I finish.

• • •

— What do you like to do for fun?

Just going out and meeting different people. Just different girls. Just talking to different girls from different places, see do all of 'em act similar. Most of 'em do. You know, sometime you try to talk to some and they won't talk to you, and then again you talk to some and they talk to you, you know, just like they like you. Most of the time I go up to that store up at the crossroads and the store on down from that. I mean, every weekend that's where I go, just talk, shoot pool if we have money, play records.

— Do you stay around your house much?

No, not much. You know, I work every day till about 3:30 now, and most of the time I don't come home till about 9:30, something like that.

I just hate to be around home by myself. I mean, Daddy, he'll be here but,

you know, I just don't like sitting around talking to him all the time. I mean, you know, he all right, but I just have to be out among young folks like me.

•   •   •

— Do you remember the happiest you've ever been?

Well, I would say it was about this girl that I was wanting to go with. And she was going with my cousin and my cousin was . . . Well, he was supposed to be something special. You know, he consider himself as being someone special, you would say. And he had this girl, she was real pretty. So I started talking to her, you know, and I convinced her that she would be better off with me than she would with him, and I got her where she kind of liked me. That made me feel real good, I was real happy about it.

How did I convince her? I told her a few stories, a little of everything. I told her about all his other girlfriends and just a whole bunch of junk. And he was kind of little, he was a lot smaller than me and, you know, everybody consider me as being small; they talk about me as being little. And my cousin's not as tall as me, and I told her — she was kind of tall too, a little taller than me, to tell you the truth — and I told her that I was taller and I would be just the right size and all that. She just thought I was just the one she was looking for. She got all crazy about me.

— Do you have a girlfriend now?

Yeah, three.

— Do you like them a lot?

One. It one that I say I like better than the other ones, but I don't exactly like her. I mean I like her, but I don't like her as I should. I mean, I don't love her, I would say, as I should. I mean, sometime I just sit down and think, do I really love her, but don't seem like I come up saying that I do.

— Have you ever been in love?

I thought I was one time. It was about three years ago, that's when I say I *thought* I was in love. It was just this girl I was going with, I had been going with her since we was in the first grade. And we went together all the way up to the ninth grade, that's when we broke up.

— Tell me about her.

What you mean, some of her ways and stuff like that? Well, I say she was good-looking, at least she was to me. She was kind of strict, she didn't want me to mess around with no other girls or nothing like that. I say she would talk too much, she tell too much about some specific things that would happen; you know, things that we did together. You know what I mean.

— You didn't ever tell anybody about things you and she did?

Not too much. I used to didn't talk too much about what was going on.

— You do now?

Right.

— Why did you change?

I don't know, I guess I just started talking more just about everything, not just that. I guess when I was smaller, I wouldn't talk much. I was kind of shy, I would say. I just wouldn't express myself how I felt or stuff like that. But a year or two ago, it changed, and now everybody say I talk too much.

— Which way do you like it?

I like it better this way, I would say. When I wasn't talking much, I didn't have but just that one girl and I didn't mess around with no others. But now I talk a lot and talk a whole bunch of trash; I just say everybody just like me now. I have more friends, I would say. Because now I talk to anybody, I don't care who it is.

— So this girl you thought you loved, why did you break up?

Well, that's about the time when I start talking a whole lot and going on and getting to be a big swinger, and she figured that after I started going down to Springer High that I had a white girlfriend. She said, "Now that you're down there, you got you a little white girl now, you ain't studying me now, you just go on and let me alone." She got mad and quit me.

— How did you feel?

Well, to tell you the truth, it hurt me pretty bad. *Then* it did. Like I just broke up or something, I don't know.

— Would you like to get back together with her?

No, I wouldn't. I think she like me now, but I don't want to go back with her. I mean, after she broke up about that, I just figured now she'll break up about any little thing now since I consider myself a big swinger.

— Tell me about the three girlfriends you've got now.

Well, I would say all of 'em about the same. None of 'em is strict or nothing like that. I say all of 'em crazy about like me. I mean, they just talk as much as me. I mean, somebody that just talk a whole bunch of junk, just call 'em crazy. Not just crazy in the head, but just crazy.

— What kind of junk do you talk?

Well, I would say if I was to tell a girl that I love her or something like that, I know I just be talking junk, talking crazy to 'em.

— Do your girlfriends go out with other boys too?

Nah. I wouldn't let 'em.

— And they let you go out with all three of them?

Right. Each girl knows that I go with the other two.

— How do they feel about that?

Well, the one that I date the most, Lorraine, she don't like it, but I guess she care enough about me not to quit me on account of it. Like if I bring up another girl's name, she'll get mad. But sometime I just be talking trash and acting crazy and I just lean over to her and say, "Oh, Connie" — that's one that I go with — "I love you so much, Connie." And she just get mad.

— What would you do if she told you she would break up with you if you didn't stop going out with the other two girls?

Just break up. Because all the other girls that I go with know that I go with every other girl, and so it don't bother them.

— Do you think it's fair not to let them go out with other boys?

In my book, I say it is because, you know, I'm a boy and you really couldn't expect no better from a boy, but you *could* from a girl.

•   •   •

— Do you plan on getting married?

Right.

— What kind of person would you like to marry?

Lorraine, I would say. I say I would marry her if she act just the way she does now and everything. I talked about it one time, but I was kidding around, I was just playing.

— What qualities would you like your wife to have?

One thing that I definitely wouldn't want is to marry one that want to follow me everywhere I go, because it's some things that I might want to do that I wouldn't want to do in front of her. Like I might want to talk to some other ladies.

— Do you plan to go out with other women when you get married?

I believe I would.

— What would you do if your wife went out with other men?

We'd just quit.

— Do you think your wife would quit you if you went out with women?

Like I say, if I marry Lorraine and she act like she do now, I don't believe she'd quit me. But she'll get mad, stay mad for about an hour or so.

— Why do you think men need women?

I would just say the main reason is to do all the housework. And for sexual desire, I guess.

•   •   •

What does my father do for a living? Well, he picks tomatoes mostly every day now. He gets sixteen cents a basket, probably averages around eight dollars a day or something like that, I don't really know. And he work down at the store every Friday.

— Is he often out of a job?

Yeah, like he might go for two or three weeks without one. See, he work on the land, and the job go down and it be a while before another one come up or something like that.

I'm working for the summer at the white school. It's a Neighborhood Youth Corps job for students who just wanna work during the summer. I mean, if the parents don't make as high a income as, you know, some of the other people, they'll give you a chance to help your own self during the summer. You know, it's just kind of a low-income type. We just do different jobs, sweep, mop, scrape paint, and pick up paper, stuff like that.

— What other type of work have you done?

Sammy Jackson

I used to pick cotton, hoe peanuts, when I was twelve. I worked back over in the fields. I just did that to help out myself, you know, just to have some spending money during the summer. I got paid about three dollars a day. Start about eight o'clock and work till about night. I just worked the summer.

And the last two summers I picked tomatoes over in Alabama. It'd take us about two hours to get there in the morning, then we'd work till about six and come on home.

— What did you think about that job?

I mean, it was okay with me because I didn't work that hard. We had girls out there picking too and we could talk to them, so it really was fun to me. We got paid about four dollars a day.

— What did you think about the pay?

That was okay with me because I was just working just to have me a little spending money of my own so I wouldn't have to ask Daddy for any money. He got most of my clothes and everything, so I didn't have nothing to worry about except just a little spending money to have on the weekends.

— Do you think you should have been paid more?

No. I mean, I made more than four dollars a day some days; that was about the average, four dollars. We got paid ten cents for every bucket we picked, so I picked about forty, you know, when there was a lot of girls around. But when it was just other boys, you know, I go on and work and get up to about six or seven dollars.

— Do you think the pay was fair for the amount of work you did?

I say it is.

— Do you believe around here black people are paid fairly by white people most of the time?

I say they is. I mean, most people say if folks don't pay 'em what they want, we won't work for 'em. So I think they usually get what they want if they work for 'em. I mean not exactly what they want, but they get around what they want, what they think the work is worth.

— How do you feel about most white people having a good deal of money and your not?

Well, it really doesn't bother me. I mean, I believe that most of 'em worked, made it. I mean, some of 'em might have cheated a little bit, but I believe most of 'em made it fair. It don't bother me too much. I mean, you know, I just don't have anything to do with it, I'd say.

— Why would you say that black people usually don't have as much as white people?

Well, I say one thing is education. Because most white people, they go to school for most of whatever job they take up. And they have a better understanding of whatever projèct they're taking up, and that way I believe they make some money.

— Whose fault is it that blacks don't have more education?

I guess I would say it was theirs, the blacks.

— Do you believe that black people would have the same chance as white people to make a lot of money if they had equal education?

I wouldn't say that they'd make just as much as the white, but I believe they would make more than they do now. Because now half of 'em don't have the proper education and by not having proper education, they just don't do as good. I mean, like the different insecticides and things like that, they might not use the proper stuff on the farm that they should and stuff like that.

— Well, why wouldn't black people make just as much if they had the same education?

Well, I just say . . . They might even make just as much. I just say that they wouldn't, but they just might, I don't know.

— Do you think education is the only reason why whites make more than blacks?

I say that's it mostly. I mean you might find a few whites every now and then that might try to gyp a black person, might try to cheat him out of a little bit, but I would say not too much now. You know, not in this day and time they wouldn't try to cheat me.

— Do you believe there's any job discrimination?

Well, I wouldn't say there is too much. I mean you might find a few places that might have job discrimination, but I wouldn't say it was that many that it would make too much difference. I would say that anywhere that a white man could get on, I figure that a black could too, most anywhere in Springer County.

•   •   •

— Did you have a lot of toys when you were little?

I say I did. I got everything I wanted for Christmas.

— What's the happiest Christmas you remember?

Well, happiest Christmas I remember was 1960 Christmas. In 1960 we got our first bicycle. And I say that was about the most enjoyable Christmas I had because we were the first boys our size to get a bicycle, and everybody else was wanting to ride it and everything. Just make me feel good, everybody coming and asking if they could ride our bicycle.

— Do you go to the doctor very often?

No, one time when I was small.

— How about the dentist?

No.

— Do you get a free lunch at school?

I used to get it free, but lately I've been paying for it, after I've been big enough to support myself, I would say. See, once while Daddy was out of a job I didn't have the money then to pay for it, and I told 'em to charge it two or three days. And so the principal called me into the office and asked me did I want to eat a free lunch and I told him okay. I started eating free lunches regular then, but after Daddy got his job back I told the principal I would be able to pay for my lunch then. I've been paying for it ever since.

• • •

— Do you consider yourself poor?

I say I would. We don't live as modernly as anybody else. I mean mostly everybody else have electricity and everything, and we don't. Mostly everybody got TV's and record players and things, and we don't.

— Does not having electricity bother you a lot?

It bothers me a lot. I mean, I just don't feel right when somebody come to see me. You know, everybody else, they have electricity and everything and we don't. So I just feel kind of shamed, I would say.

— How would you go about getting electrical wires back in here?

It could be easy done, I don't see why Daddy haven't done it. He could have it run down here. I've told him about it. Ever since I've been big enough to feel we should have it, I've been talking to him about it. But he said he gon build him a house on this land because the Jackson family owns it. And he's been putting it off.

— Where do you get your water?

We get water from over to the next house about a mile away. We usually get it in the car when the car running, but when it's not, we walk.

— How do you feel about having to haul your water down here?

Well, I hate it. I mean, I just hate to be walking up and down the road hauling water. I mean, I just don't feel right about it, feel shamed.

— Where do you go to the bathroom?

We go out back of the house, just use the woods.

— How do you feel about that?

I hate that part. I just hate going in the woods. And I would hate an out-door toilet too. One thing I say the woods is not so sanitary.

— Has your father ever complained about being poor?

No. I don't never hear him saying nothing about it, that's the part that bothers me. I mean, maybe if he felt the same way I do about it, he'd go on and do something about it in a hurry and make better progress.

— And how do you feel about it?

Well, just like I say, I just feel shamed about it; I just hate the whole part.

— If your father felt the same way, what could he do to improve the situation?

I think that if he felt the same way I did about it, he'd go on and build him another house.

— Does he have enough money to build a house?

Well, I wouldn't say he have enough now, but he did have enough last year when he was doing construction work, I believe.

— What would you say is the cause of your being poor?

Well, I say really it's not caring. That's the way I would put it, he just don't care. I mean Daddy, he grew up like that, just grew up ordinarily. When he was small he didn't have any electricity and stuff like that, so I guess it just didn't matter too much to him after he got older.

•   •   •

— Do you get commodity food?

Right.

— What do you think of it?

Well, that don't bother me too much, because a lot of people better off than we are still get it. I wouldn't say the food, it doesn't bother me so bad.

— Do you feel the national government is good or bad for most poor people?

I would say it's too good for some of 'em. I mean, the welfare is helping all these people that don't really need help. In some ways I see where it is right, helping people that can't help themselves, but just supporting all these lazy folks, got these babies and all that, I don't like it. Especially when they won't work. You know, able and everything, just living off the government. And they just spending up other people's money; all the ones that working, all the taxpayers and folks like that, it's their money.

•   •   •

— Do you think that when you get older you'll be well off?

Right. I mean, I'm just determined since I live so poor all my life just to make somebody out of myself, have mostly everything I want. Really, I'll just say I'll try to get a good education. Most days now, if you get a good education, you can get a good job.

— What would you like to do for a job?

I haven't thought about it too hard, but I believe I would like to read computers or something like that. I decided that because we took some kind of test at school, and it came out that I would be better reading some kind of computer or something like that. So I just gave it some thought and it seem like I might would like that kind of job.

— Before the test, what kind of work did you want to do?

Teaching.

　　　　　　　・　　　・　　　・

— What's the worst thing about Springer County?

I'll say the worst thing to me is it's so small and nothing to do. It's just not enough town, I would say.

— Would you like to move?

I wouldn't mind moving but, you know, I would hate moving. But I wouldn't care so bad.

— But if you had a choice, you wouldn't move to a bigger city?

I would. In some ways I'd want to and some ways I just wouldn't want to move. I mean, I would just hate to leave out from around here, just leave the people, you know, some friends. But I plan to move from here when I get out of high school. I have two or three reasons. One reason is not enough jobs to make a fair living down here, take care of your problems. Another reason because, you know, mostly everybody that finishes school with me and everything, they leaving. Go looking. You know, you just wouldn't want to be the only one out of the bunch that would stay around after all of 'em leaving.

— Do you like the city better than the country?

I wouldn't say so. I like the country better. I mean out in the country you just have more room or more privacy to do whatever you want to, but in the city everything is so crowded. I just wouldn't like it as good as I would in the country.

— Would you stay in the country if there were job opportunities and recreational facilities here?

I believe I would. I mean, just going to the city, it really doesn't mean anything. If I could get a good job and everything down here, I would just stay on down.

— Where do you plan to move?

First I'll probably go to Newark, New Jersey, stay about a month or two. I just might stay up there for good, but I know definitely that I'll probably stay about a month or so. See, I got relatives up there, and I could kind of be around there and they might help me out a little bit. And then after they might give me a little money, then I can move on to wherever I wanna go. But I would like to stay somewhere up near Newark and New York probably. I mean, mostly everybody that leave out from down here, that's mostly where they go.

— Do any of them ever come back down here and tell you how things are up there?

Right. We have people coming for Christmas holidays and Fourth of July. They come back and they tell us how it is up there and everything. They said it's all right, and you can easily find a good job, but they say everything up there is pretty high and you have to have a right large sum income to live on the average.

— Do you recognize any difference between them and the people who have been living here all their lives?

Some of 'em I do and some of 'em I don't. Some of 'em will leave and come back the same, but some have more after they leave and stay awhile than they did when they was down here.

And most of 'em, their skin change, their skin color. I mean, you can take one real dark and they'll leave and stay a certain length of time and they just come like light skin. And they change in talk. While they're down here they just talk flat, just natural country talk, but after they get up there they just have that northern accent.

.   .   .

— What is the most terrifying thing you've ever seen happen?

Well, I say going to the moon, the astronauts going to the moon. I mean, I didn't disbelieve it, but it was real terrifying just looking at them on TV, landing and everything. Just all those holes and things, craters, it just terrifying to me.

— Would you like to have been the first man to step on the moon?

No. Do you believe they went?

— Yes, I guess I do. Do you believe it?

Yeah, I believe they went. I hear heap of people say they didn't go to God's moon — they'll always put that in there every time — they didn't go to God's moon. But I believe they went.

.   .   .

— Do you ever feel lonely?

Uh-huh. Most times it just when I get down and start daydreaming, I would say, just thinking hard.

— What are you thinking about?

Well, I just think about a bunch of things. I think about my brother, I think about Mama sometimes, think about my girlfriend, and all that added together just makes me feel lonely, I guess.

.   .   .

— When you were little, did you ever envy white children?

I didn't envy them, but sometime when I was small I just say I wish I was white. I'd just be talking with different small boys, I said I wish I was white.

— How did it come up?

I mean, you might walk around and see 'em with money all the time, or they might have a good swing set or something like that and we didn't have it, we just say we wish we was white and get everything that we wanted.

— Do you still wish you were white?

No.

— Why did you change?

I don't know why, I just changed, I guess. I mean, me and some of the white boys at school just be sitting around talking sometimes, and I just be kidding around talking and just say no matter how hard I wish I could be white, I could never change, my color would never change.

— Why do you say that to them?

I just be talking bullshit.

— Which term do you prefer — Negro, black, or colored?

Black. I just like the word *black*. *Negro,* it just don't mean nothing. You know, we just don't go around calling the white man a different name, we just call him white like he is. So I'd just rather go on and be called black like I am.

•   •   •

— Describe the difference, if you see any, between black and white people.

Let me see. Well, I would say about the income part, it's some difference. You know, all the whites try to live just as good as they can, get everything they want; I mean, some of 'em have a heap of things they really don't need, but because they wanted 'em, they got 'em. A lot of black folks, I would say, just wouldn't care, don't make any difference with them.

— Do you think black people could do everything as well as white people if given the chance?

Yes, I believe they could. I just believe it because I would say from experience that a heap of blacks I know could do some jobs that whites can't do as good. Like auto mechanicing. Like on the school bus one time, we had a little fan that keeps the driver cool to tear up. So the driver took it to different white mechanics around town, but couldn't any of 'em fix it. And then he took it to this boy — he was black — and he worked on it for about ten minutes and fixed it.

— So you think there's something about black people that makes them better mechanics?

I would say so. I would say it is just born in 'em to be good at whatever they take up. But I would say all the whites that take up jobs, they take 'em up because they like 'em. What I mean is, say, like you was to take up teaching. I would just say you took up that job because you just like teaching. But I would say that a black person that took up mechanics didn't take it up because they liked it; it was just born in 'em to be good at stuff like that. And they might go to school and get a better education at it, but some of 'em don't even go to school.

•   •   •

— How do most black people in this area act around whites?

Most of 'em, they act kind of scary toward 'em. I mean, if one says something to you and you know it's not right and they know it too, most blacks won't say anything about it.

— Do you think younger people or older people are more afraid?

Older. It might not just be that they are more scarier, but it's the way it seems. I know it's some boys I go to school with, I say *yeah* and *no* to 'em, and I know some grownups say *yassir* and *naw sir* to 'em. It just don't make sense to me. Older people see me saying *yeah* and *no* to 'em in front of their face, and then they turn around and say *yassir* and *naw sir* to 'em and call 'em mister, and it just don't make sense to me. It seems to me they scared of 'em or something, I don't know. They say they ain't scared, just showing respect for 'em.

Yeah, me and my daddy think different on this. He say I should say *yes sir* and *no sir* to a white person just as quick as I would to a black person, and I agree with him on that. And I do say it to grown white people just like I do black. But white children, they won't say *yes sir* and *no sir* to your parents, but they looking for you to say it to theirs.

— Have you ever talked back to whites?

The janitor we work with, if he tell me something that I don't like, I tell him about it. Me and another boy, we was slinging weeds for a whole week and we come back up to the schoolhouse when we finished and we were sweeping and stuff like that. And so we were mopping the lunchroom and it took us forty-five minutes the first day to do it. And the janitor told us if we didn't finish quicker he was gon put us back out there in the sun doing hard work because we didn't need to do no easy work if we couldn't do it and go on and get through with it. And I just told him how I felt about it. I told him before I go back down there, I'll just quit. I told him to hell with him and that damned sun out there.

And one time I talked at the principal. See, there's this bus driver — he black — he been at me for a long time. And about two months ago, there was some boys at the back of the bus cussing and talking a whole bunch of trash at him. And I was sitting back there with 'em and he thought it was me and he sat up there and he called me a whole bunch of names. And I went up there and asked him what he was talking about, why didn't he quit running his mouth and talking about me all the time, why didn't he get up if he wanted to whip me. So he just hushed.

Then the next morning he went and told the principal a whole bunch of stories, made like I cut up on the bus, take my time getting on and off, that I pick at everybody, like that. And the principal was just saying I did all these things, and I got mad and I start talking at the principal, you know, just raising my voice at him and stuff like that to show him I was mad. And I asked him how come he never ask me what's going on, how come he didn't ask me what happened. He got mad, told me never to come to his office like that. He said next time I do it, I just find another school to go to.

· · ·

— Did your father ever tell you anything about race?

Not any that I remember.

— If you have children, will you teach them anything about race?

No. I wouldn't say I would teach 'em, I guess they would just grow up with it in 'em. You know, grow up with it, know how they should act, I mean. If somewhere they step out of line, you know, think that they should do something they shouldn't like going around meddling with white kids and saying things to 'em that they shouldn't, then I would talk to 'em about it.

— When you were a small child, how did you feel about not being able to go in restaurants and things?

Well, when I was little, it just never occurred to me, I just never thought it was any of my business. I mean, it just never crossed my mind.

— Are there any places where you can't go now?

Well, I would say the restaurant in Shady Grove. I mean, I don't never see nobody go in; they say you can go in the back part and order what you want, but you can't go around to the front part. But one day a lady sent me there to get something and I was fixing to go in, but another lady told me she would go for it.

But I'm going in there when I get me some money. Going in the front. There's this white boy I work with, he'd go to the restaurant after we finished work, and I'd just tell him, "If I had enough money, I'd go in there and get me a plate right with you." But the first week we started to work I didn't have enough

money to go in and order what I want like a good plate or something. And so me and two or three other boys, black friends, we talked about it and we said we gon do it one day. You know, just go in there. See, we were talking about it because we had this boy that played on the baseball team, he's black and he's the one that won the state championship for us because he could pitch real good. And after the big game, all the rest of the team went down to this restaurant, but this boy that was the pitcher didn't go. And we said, "Old Wallace ought to go down and eat lunch with the rest of the boys. He play on the team and everybody else like him so good, so he just ought to go to the restaurant and get him a plate with the rest of the boys."

— Don't you have enough money now to go to the restaurant?

I mean, I have some, but . . . I just haven't went in there I would say I'm planning on it.

— What are some other examples of discrimination and prejudice you know of?

I would say that's about all.

— What changes would you like to see in white people as a whole?

I wouldn't say none. I mean, they can stay just like they is now, for me.

— Why do you think some whites think they're better than blacks?

I couldn't answer that, because you find that most of the whites in this town that are kind of wealthy, they're just as nice and everything . . . But you find one that's kind of poor — not exactly poor, but not as wealthy as some of the wealthy ones — they try to be Mister It. I mean, they just don't dig black folks. You know, you might just walk by their house or something like that, they won't say nothing to you. But you walk by some of the wealthy folks' house, they'll speak to you and stuff like that there.

— How do you think whites keep the power?

Well, I say that they just keep a white man in office just because he's white. I mean, you have some black people in government but not as many as whites. But I figure like this here: If a white man sees a white man, he'll vote for him quicker than he would a black man because he was black. I guess some blacks do the same thing; they vote for a black man whether he qualified or not, just because he black.

• • •

— What do you think about intermarriage between blacks and whites?

What do I think about it? Well, really, it doesn't bother me. It just left up to the people that getting married; I mean if they feel they love each other enough to make it through like things are now, it's up to them.

— Would you marry a white woman?

I would say living in Shady Grove I wouldn't. Things would be too rough on me. There ain't no telling what would happen, they just probably kill me and blow up my house and stuff like that.

•   •   •

— Do you learn things about famous black people in school?

Not too much, but some. We learned about a famous black man that was the first one to shed blood on American soil during the Revolutionary War that night they was throwing all those snowballs at the British soldiers. And Frederick Douglass, he's one we discussed. And a history book talked about Dr. Martin Luther King, Jr., and Roy Wilkins and Benjamin Mays and different people like that.

— Did you like learning about them?

Right. Sometime some of the things make you kind of feel stupid, but it was really fun. I mean after it was over with, it was. But sometimes you feel kind of stupid. Like sometime you see old pictures in the book of black people from way back and slaves and things that make you look . . . Just make you feel ashamed about yourself. And those films we saw in the seventh grade on slavery, it just tickle you, it just kind of funny to you or something. We might see some old slave, see him out there in the field, working and sweating, you see their master standing around with whips in their hands. I say it just kind of funny now, just make you feel kind of funny.

— Did the film say slavery was bad or good?

Well, some of it showed some good points and some of it showed some bad points. It showed where some blacks owned slaves themselves, it said some of the slaves had nice masters, they freed 'em their own selves after the war and tried to help 'em get away and showed several that didn't want to free the slaves. And it show sometime where a slave had been disobedient to his master and they had him tied up where they was whipping him. And some of the places where they was staying, I would say they weren't so good.

— What did the teacher say about slavery?

Well, she was against slavery. Yeah, she was white — this was at the white school — and she said she didn't think it was right for people to be working human beings as animals. Some of the kids sometimes would make a wisecrack, like they might say, "Old Sammy need to be my slave, I'll work him to death," or something like that. I was the only black student in the class.

— What did you think about that?

Well, it just kind of tickled me, because I don't think now it possible that I would become their slave. So it was just kind of funny to me, and they were just joking and everything.

· · ·

— What percentage of whites in Springer County do you think are prejudiced?

I say about 10 or 20 percent. That's the way that I feel about it, about 10 or 20 percent.

— How did you arrive at that figure?

Just by some of the things I hear. Just by hearing people talk about what such and such a person said.

I'm Somebody Important

— What would you think if someone told you he thought about 90 percent were prejudiced?

I would just say I wouldn't believe there was that many. That's just what I say about it. I wouldn't argue with 'em, you know, I'd just say I didn't feel there was that many.

— What if you found out there were that many?

I'd just feel let down, I would say, been fooled or something like that. I'd just be let down in just having more confidence in 'em by the way, you know, the children at school act and everything.

•   •   •

— Do you think the racial situation has changed during the past five years?

I believe it has. I would say we are getting along now better than we is in the past five years. You know, about the places that we used to couldn't go to, we can go to now. Stuff like that. And I would say that some change.

— Is integration important to you?

I wouldn't say it would be important, but I believe it would better things, you know, make things better. Because as long as we don't have it, we just keep up confusion and riots and things like that. But now that we're integrating I would say that we is beginning to understand each other better, that we can get along better.

— Did going to the white school change your attitudes toward whites in any way?

I would say so. Before I went, I always thought that they was real mean, big fighters. You know, I thought they was always wanting to fight all the time, or cuss at you, be real nasty to you all the time. But I found out different.

— What further changes would you like to see in the relations between whites and blacks?

Well, one thing I would like to see is for just all of 'em, just right around in Springer County, just really mixing up. I mean just really mixing up in things they do. You know, like if they have some kind of big event or something like that, I'd like to see 'em just really mix up, all of 'em together and just talking together and laughing together and everything.

— Do you believe it will ever happen?

I believe it will eventually. I would say I believe it'll be that way in about the next five years or next two or three.

Well, I couldn't say how it would come about, but I just believe it will. I mean, if they have anything together now, all of 'em be standing out together, but sometimes it might not be talking and going on. But all of 'em together, and I believe if they keep that up, it'll just change; they just be going and talking to each other and all that.

• • •

— Would you like a civil rights organization in Shady Grove?

I believe I would.

— Why?

I say it's just because it's a civil rights group, I guess.

— What is it about a civil rights group that makes you want one here?

Well, they said that the civil rights group help you out if they have any trouble and everything.

— Have you ever thought about that, that you wish there was one here?

No, I ain't never thought about it.

— Would you join?

I doubt it, probably wouldn't.

— Why not?

I just wouldn't.

— You must have some reasons.

I mean, sometimes groups like that can get too rough, you know, start riots and stuff like that, and really I wouldn't want to be in one. I mean, just for nothing. I mean if the riot was peaceful and worthwhile, it'd be all right, but just for looting and stuff like that, I wouldn't want to be in it.

— Have you heard of these groups? NAACP?

Yes. To tell you the truth, I don't know nothing about 'em, I just heard talk of 'em.

— SCLC?

Uh-huh. I don't know nothing about it exactly, but isn't that the group that Dr. Martin Luther King was with? What I heard and mostly that I saw of all the stuff they did, they did it peacefully and not a whole bunch of rioting and stuff like that.

— The Black Panthers?

Yeah, I heard talk about that. Just from what I read and heard people say, they definitely don't like white folks.

— What do you think of the Panthers?

Well, if they just hate white folks and go around and jump on 'em just for the fun of it, I wouldn't think that's right. I think they shouldn't do it if that's just what they do.

— What do you think about trying to bring about change by burning and bombing?

Well, I wouldn't exactly agree to that. I mean, if a man owned this big restaurant or something and he didn't want any blacks coming to his place, I just say that's him, it's his place; if he don't want 'em, that's him, that's left up to him. If he don't want to be fooling around with 'em, what's the use of going in there and trying to tear up his place? Just bump it, just leave him alone. That's the way I figured it out.

— What did you think about Dr. King?

Well, I think he was all right, he was a pretty good man. One thing from what I read, he was one of the first ones to start picketing about wanting these colored — I mean these black — people to sit down on the bus; they had this certain section where black people had to sit and if that section was filled up they had to stand up. He picketed so folks could ride that bus. I say that was some good he did. And they say he did a whole bunch of stuff in Atlanta. I say that was some of the good things that he done, doing peaceful riots if they was necessary.

— What do the white students at your school think of King?

Well, most of 'em, they don't like him. When they had his funeral, when they was burying him, they just had a whole bunch of smart junk to say and stuff like that. Like, "Well, I'm glad he's dead," and all that kind of stuff. "He wasn't no good," and all that.

About two weeks before he got killed they showed a picture of him on TV or in the book and one boy said, "I wish he was dead." About two more weeks from then, you know after he got killed, I asked the boy did he still feel the same way about him. He said yes.

— And what did you say?

Nothing. I just said, "That's just the sense you got. How would you feel now if it was some of your kin people and somebody said something about him like that?" He didn't say nothing.

— Did any of them ever say anything else about him and you said you disagreed?

Uh-huh. I mean, if they were to say anything about him that I didn't think was right, I tell 'em they was wrong. Like they would say he started all these riots and stuff like that. I tell 'em that he didn't and stuff like that.

— What did they say to you?

They just asked me why I was like that, trying to take up for him all the time.

— And what did you say?

I say, "Well, he ain't did nothing wrong, what's the use of me hating him for? He ain't did nothing to me."

∙　∙　∙

— What's the most exciting thing that ever happened to you?

I'll say one important thing that I'd say was real exciting, that was when we first got our car. We got it Easter Saturday before last. Well, we was up to our uncle's house in Charlestown spending the weekend with him, and Daddy had told us that Thursday before we left that he was gon see could he get a car. And he went to Alcoa that Saturday, and he got one. And he didn't have his license at that time and he had another lady we knew drive it for him. And she drove back over there to my uncle's that Saturday evening. You know, we wasn't really expecting too much for him to get a car. So she come driving up and we didn't see Daddy in it, but we knew it was our car when we first saw it because we knew she didn't have one. So we run out there where it was and Daddy was laying down in the car. He was hiding from us, you know, to keep us from knowing that it was ours; he was just surprising us, you know.

I'd say that was about the most important thing that ever happened, but when I first went to the fair I thought that was really exciting, riding around on everything. It was when I was smaller, about seven or eight. And we had been working all the week picking cotton, pick about ten or twenty pounds a day. About the end of that week me and my brother had about two or three dollars, you know, just our money, just our little money. We went down there that Saturday night, and, you know, when we have a little money like that when we was small, we thought we had everything then. We rode around, eat popcorn, stuff like that, and I thought it was real exciting because it was my first fair.

∙　∙　∙

— How would you describe yourself?

Can it be something stupid? I would just say the little love-man. Everybody call me little, but yet I just say I'm just real popular with the girls.

∙　∙　∙

— Have you had any big problems in growing up?

Yeah, I would say walking is one. When I was doing all that walking before we got our car, that was one problem. I mean, everywhere I wanted to go, we

had to walk. Like if we going to town, we start out walking, and if we didn't catch us a ride, we just walk. And we just walked to church.

•　　•　　•

— When do you feel the most alive?

I would say when I get right up on some girls.

— How do you feel then?

Well, look like I just change all of a sudden, look like I just feel really alive, just feel real good, and just feel like I just want to talk a whole bunch of trash. We just talk a lot; I would just say tempt 'em. You know how you tempt people? When you tempt people, just playing with her, not just walking around hitting on each other and running, but just talking to 'em and fooling 'em and stuff like that there.

— Do you think girls like you pretty much?

I would think so.

— Why?

Well, I asked another boy that question Monday. He just said he would believe it was because I was crazy and in the way I dress.

— What did he mean by crazy?

Just talking a whole bunch of junk and stuff like that.

— Pretend I'm a girl and talk some junk for me.

I can't do it. I just can't do it. I just change when I meet some girls.

— Do you change when you get around white girls?

I wouldn't say exactly the same, but I change. I don't talk as much junk around them as I do black girls.

•　　•　　•

— If you could have three wishes come true, what would they be?

A house and everything it have with it, like TV's and stove. And get me a good car, just my own car. That Mama was living.

•　　•　　•

— What's your biggest dream?

Well, one of my biggest dreams is that I would like to be somebody important.

— What type of important?

Well, it really wouldn't matter with me. I mean, I just wanna be somebody important, something like some big man. I wanna become somebody famous.

— Do you ever think of what you would want to be or what you'd want to do?

Not really. But I have thought pretty seriously about discovering something, you know, something new that haven't ever been discovered before.

— Why do you want to be someone important?

I would say that one reason is because my brother said he would like to be somebody kind of important, and I thought about it kind of seriously and after he left I still thought about it. You know, he said he wasn't too smart in his books and everything. And there was this teacher, he was kind of hard on him, tried to throw off on him all the time, trying to embarrass him in the classroom. He just said he wanted to be someone important. So I just figured that since I was poor all my life I would just like to be somebody to just show 'em that I could be a man, you know. And in my work, everybody just say I be the sorriest one out of my family, you know. And I just wanna be somebody to show 'em different.

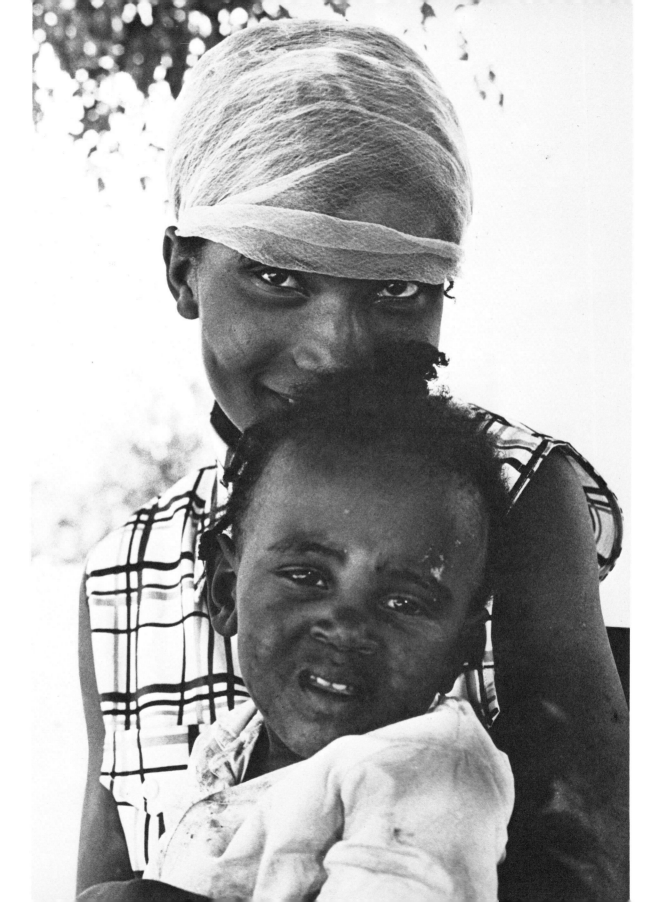

Rosie Mae Davis

Rosie Mae Davis, a very quiet girl of eighteen, spends a lot of her time holding her two-year-old baby in her lap. She is not married, so she lives with her family about six miles from Shady Grove. The only outsiders who pass through this secluded town are fun-seekers on their way to a nearby lake, and shiny cars pulling speedboats often whiz by Rosie Mae's unpainted house. Rosie Mae is shy, and although she appeared to enjoy the interviews, she would cover her face with her hands while answering a question, and sometimes she would sit silently for minutes before saying anything.

    — What's something good that has happened to you?

    . . . I'm kind of 'shamed to tell you; I'm kind of shy to tell you.

    — What would you think about my leaving for a minute and your saying it with the tape recorder on?

    Yeah, I would like that.

    . . . Good thing I have a baby.

•   •   •

When we was living right up the road up there, we didn't hardly have nothing to eat. I was about twelve. It went on about seven or eight months. See, my father, he was working at the peanut mill and so they turned some of the hands off, and he couldn't hardly find another job.

— How did you feel being hungry?

I get hungry I get sick. I just felt like I was gon die. I thought I was, I was so hungry.

— What would you do?

I'll lay down. I'll lay down all day just about. I was so weak and sick I couldn't hardly walk.

— Did you get some food every day?

I ate a piece of meat. Some hog meat.

— Did you get some every day?

Not every day. Some days I wouldn't have nothing to eat. But we got some meat. My daddy helped a man kill some hogs. And for that, he got some meat. We ate off that for about three weeks, maybe longer than that. And sometimes get meal.

— Did you all talk about your situation?

We be saying we wish we had some better than this or we wish we had more than this. You know, we say we get tired of eating that meat all the time, wouldn't have nothing else. Finally, Daddy, he got him a job. Got him a job working on the road. We felt all right then. We felt like we usually feel.

— During this time did you go to school?

I wouldn't go when I was hungry. I was sick and hungry. I stayed out about a month, then I started back to going.

— Were you still hungry when you started back to school?

Uh-huh, I felt weak and sick some. I don't think they was giving free lunches then. So I feel, still feel the same, sick.

•   •   •

I can read just a little bit, not much. I have sort of a hard time reading. See, I wouldn't learn all that much in school. The teacher, she be carrying on with the other children's lessons, she wouldn't even much carry me on in a lesson or nothing. The teacher be teaching other children, but she wouldn't say nothing to me. Looked like she asked them questions, something or nuther, and they answered, and she wouldn't ask me nothing. It was that way in all the grades. They would help me some at the white school, but they wouldn't at the colored.

— How did you read your school books and do your homework and pass tests and everything?

How would I do it? I wouldn't do it. I wouldn't do any reading. I would let my brother help me with my homework.

— Did you cheat on your tests?

Yeah, I do that a heap of times.

— Why didn't you ask the teacher to help you?

She acted like she didn't want to pay me no attention, that's the reason I didn't do it.

•　　•　　•

— Which word do you prefer — black, Negro, or colored?

Colored. Because some white people around here use *nig-ger*. I'll say all of 'em use the word *nigger,* ole nigger.

They've called me one — a lot. When I used to go to school with 'em. Some of 'em call me ole nigger. Some of 'em say, "Ole nigger, don't sit side of me."

Yeah, I went to the white school. I went to the colored school first and then I went to the white school. I got tired of the colored teachers whipping me, you know, so I decided I would change and go to the white school.

Uh-huh, I got whipped a lot in the colored school. Sometimes be about my lessons and sometimes about fighting. Sometimes me and some girls be playing and don't get our lessons, and the teacher whip us about it. And sometimes they would whip you for not doing good on a test. Sometime I do good and sometimes I won't and then they'll whip me, I'd go to crying.

And sometimes I get a whipping for nothing; children tell stories on me. I wouldn't be doing nothing and they just tell a story and put my name on the board, and when the teacher come back he'll whip me. Sometimes this girl named Katie Davis — like the teacher go out — she just put my name on the board and teacher come back, he'll whip me. The teacher always got her to take names. Ole Katie put my name on the board, I tell her, "Katie, what you wanna put my name on the board for and make me get a whipping?" She wouldn't say nothing then. This was the seventh grade. I was kind of afraid to do something to her — see, her father was the principal, and I was kind of afraid she would go back and tell him.

— Do you remember the worst whipping you ever got in school?

Yeah. The teacher whipped me and swole my hand up so *big*. Hit me with a strap, swole my whole arm up.

But the white teachers don't whip you. Just like you do something, they punish you, they expel you from school for about a week.

I was starting the ninth grade when I signed up to go to the white school. The first day I went, it was kind of all right. The second day I went, the white children started picking at me then. Calling me nigger and things. Girls and boys, about five of 'em, would come over and say, "Look at this ole nigger, I don't want this ole nigger sitting side of me."

— How did that make you feel?

Well, I felt 'shamed they calling me nigger.

— Did this keep up the whole time you were there?

Naw, it didn't keep up the whole time I was there. They stopped; they started but they stopped. They did it for about two months and they quit. Because I started getting 'em told. When they came over to me and called me old nigger, I would say, "Shut up talking to me, honky," that's what I would say. They wouldn't say nothing then. It was about five that would call me nigger. When I started calling them a honky, they stopped calling me a nigger. After that, they wouldn't say nothing to me and I wouldn't say nothing to them.

— Before you signed up for the white school, did you think that the students might call you a nigger?

Yeah. I just said I guess them white children gon call me a nig-ger. I told my mama. She said, "That's what you get for signing up to go."

— Were there any white students there you liked?

One. I liked a girl named Gladys Norris all right. She wouldn't never pick at me, act always nice to me. Like she liked to go around with me a lot, you know, in school. And sometimes when I wouldn't know something, she would help me.

— Did you ever invite her home?

No. I liked her all right in school, but not asking home.

— Which school did you like better, the colored or the white?

When they stopped picking at me, the white. They didn't whip you at the white school and you have a better time at the white school than the colored. The reason I liked it, most of the time we would have homemaking, and we have a nice time doing that, cooking and all.

— How long were you at the white school?

About seven or eight months, and then I stopped. When I dropped out, I was with my baby — that was the reason I dropped out. They told me I could have went on, but I just didn't want to go. Because I real 'shamed to keep going, and I start feeling bad.

• • •

I wanted to have a baby.

— Why?

Because I just like to have one. I just wanted to have a baby.

— Did you get pregnant by accident or on purpose?

On purpose.

— Did you want to get married?

Yeah.

— Did you think you were going to get married before you got pregnant?

Well, the boy that messed me up — his name Junior — he left after he did it. We never had talked none about getting married. I just want the baby. When I told him I was gon have a baby, he just told me a story he *didn't* do it, but I know he did it. I told him he *did* do it.

— How did you feel when he said he wasn't the father?

I felt awful. Mad, too. I jumped on him and me and him got to fighting. I started hitting him. He didn't hit me back though.

— What happened then?

He left town then. I never have seen him none since then. He ain't never come back.

— How would you feel if he did come back?

I'd jump on him again because he did me like that. Try to slap him, hit him.

— How did you feel about him before you got pregnant?

I loved him. I had been going with him about two years.

— Do you think about him very often now?

I think about him sometime. I think about I wish he would come, I'd like to see him. Because I still love him.

— But you said if he came back, you'd jump on him again. Would you?

Uh-huh. And love him, too.

— Tell me about meeting him.

The first time I ever seen him, he was up to the store. He was standing up to the counter. So I walked up to the counter where he was. I asked him what was his name and he told me and then I told him I loveded him. And then he told me he loveded me, so we started in together.

He was the only one I went out with till Michelle was born, just him. Because he had it some kind of better than the others. And he's still the only one I care about.

— What was it about him that made you love him?

Because he was pretty.

— Do you go out with boys now?

Uh-huh. I have seven boyfriends right now. We go up there to that old juke, and sometimes go to the club. I like 'em but don't just straight out love 'em.

— Would you marry any of them?

No.

— Do you want to get married?

I ain't thinking about getting married, not now.

— Could you do without men all your life?

No. If you do without, that's when you soon go crazy.

— Do most of the boys around here like you a lot?

Uh-huh.

— Why?

Because . . . I'm kind of 'shamed to tell it. I guess because . . . I'm kind of 'shamed to tell that. I guess because I have something good for 'em.

— Do many boys tell you you're pretty?

Uh-huh. I tell 'em I ain't pretty. I'm ugly.

— Do you think you're ugly?

I don't know. I guess I look all right, I reckon.

•   •   •

After about four months after I got pregnant I stopped going to school. And my mother didn't know I was pregnant. I hadn't told her because I was kind of shy to tell her, I thought she was gon whip me. So she started whipping me because I wouldn't go to school. And I'd run out the house, and then when I come back in, I kind of scared to tell her. And then I told her. I thought she was gon whip me but she didn't. She just said, "Whose is it?" I said, "Junior's."

— What does your mother think of Junior now?

She might hate him now, I don't know.

— Have you ever told her you still love him?

Uh-huh, many times. Way it'll come up she'll go to talking about how the baby looks like him. Then I say, "I still love him." She'll say, "Like he did you, you ought not to still love him." That's what she'll say. I'll say, "Aw, foot, I wanted a baby." She'll tell me to hush my mouth.

— Did you tell your father you were pregnant?

No, I didn't tell Daddy. He found it out when I started getting bigger. He just said, "That gal done went and got her gut stuck out."

•   •   •

I was real happy when I had Michelle. I was real happy. And Mama was real happy too. She say, "I got me a little granddaughter."

— What would you think if you got pregnant again?

I hope I don't get like that no more. But I wouldn't think nothing. If I done got messed up, ain't nothing I can do. I just wanted to have Michelle but I

don't want nary'n nuther. You have a time birthing 'em. You have a hard time when you getting in labor. It feel like you going to die or something. You be hurting real bad.

— What hopes do you have for Michelle?

I hope when she get up a big girl she wouldn't have no baby. I would teach her not to have nary'n. I'd teach her not to have none when she's sort of little, wait till she get grown to have some.

— Do you wish you didn't have her at your age?

I've thought to say that sometime. Because sometime I like to go out and sometime Mama don't like to keep the baby.

— Does you mother help you much with Michelle?

Yeah. Like sometime she be sick and have a cold or something or nuther, she get her medicine, stuff like that. And like picking up some asafetida or something or nuther. You never seen any asafetida? It's some kind of white stuff, kind of like balls, you give it to 'em to teethe 'em, you know. Put it in a rag and tie it around their necks.

Uh-huh, my mama spanks Michelle. She spanks her the most because she all the time be whipping on Jimmy Frank — he's my brother, he about seven. She bites him. She just kind of mean. She bites me sometimes.

— What do you think about your mother spanking her?

I think she *should* spank her.

— Do you spank her much?

I spank her sometime for biting and making water in her clothes. Sometimes I make her go outdoors and make water. Then she will let me know when she gets ready to do it.

— Does your mother tell you how to raise Michelle?

Yeah, she tells me what to do. Sometimes like when Michelle be whipping on Jimmy Frank, she tell me, "You ought to beat that baby and raise her better than that." Sometimes I won't be feeling like beating her.

•　　•　　•

My daddy's not my real one. He's my stepfather.

—Where is your real father?

I don't know. I never did know him.

— When did your mother and real father separate?

They weren't married. My mother was married to my stepfather.

— Do you ever think about who your real father was?

Huh-uh.

— Are your parents strict?

I don't know . . . I don't know what that means.

— Have they set down a lot of rules for you through the years and whipped you if you didn't follow them?

Uh-huh, they were. Sometimes when I'd slip off, when I come back they would whip me. I was about thirteen, I'd slip off at night. I'd hoist the window and get out the window. I would sneak out to go see Junior. We'd meet in this barn. He would tell me when he gon be there so I'd know what time. So I'd go to the barn then. We wouldn't stay long, and then I would sneak back in the window.

Sometimes they would be in bed and wouldn't know I'd gone. Sometimes they'll catch me. They would say, "I know you done went out and met Junior." That what they'd say. And I'd say, "Huh-uh, no I didn't." That's what I'd say. They'll say, "Don't tell no story now, I know you did." I say, "Huh-uh, no I didn't."

— How often did you get whippings when you were little?

I would get whippings regular when I was little. Sometimes about going to the spring and toting in wood. They'd want us to tote in wood, and they'd whip us and make us do it. And sometimes they'd whip us about not going to the spring to get some water. Sometimes when we was little and we didn't want to go to school, they'd whip us about that.

— Do your parents ever fight?

Yeah, they used to when I was about seven or eight. I'd tell 'em to quit that and don't do it no more. I'd say it to my daddy, tell him not to hit her no more. I'd say, "Daddy, don't hit Mother no more, you'll hurt her."

•　　•　　•

I have three whole brothers and three half-brothers and five half-sisters. See, my daddy had some before he married Mama. The ones that live here at home — all of 'em are brothers — I've got one six and one nineteen and one twenty. Six live here . . . Seven, I guess. The others don't live here. I have three sisters in Hartford, Connecticut, and I have one live in Florida.

And I had a little sister and two brothers that died. I had one died in 1959. I wasn't born when the others died. But I was about seven or eight when my brother died. I don't know what happened, he just took sick all at once and died. He was thirteen months old. I went to crying. I *loved* to play with him. I said, "Mama" — his name was Robert — I said, "Robert dead?" She said, "Uh-huh." I started crying.

•　　•　　•

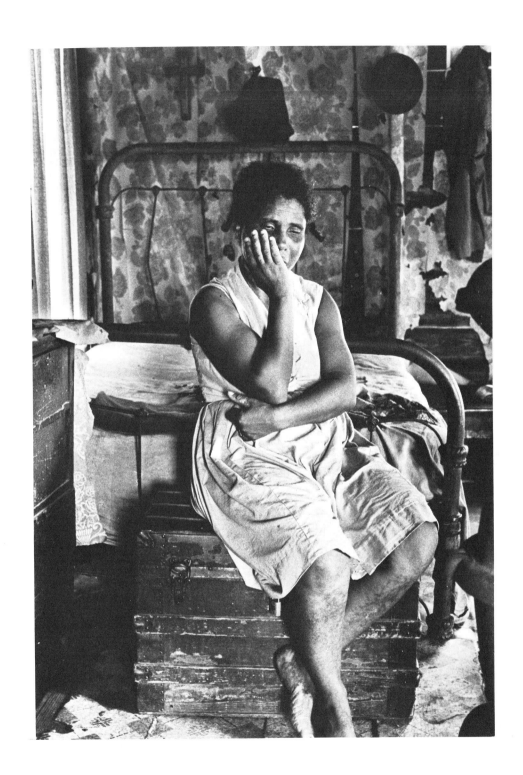

I picked cotton when I was about seven up until I was about thirteen. Mama, she would give us a little something for picking. We picked but she'd get the money. Sometimes I tell her I want the money. She'd say, "I ain't gon give it it to you." I'd tell her, "Sometimes I ain't gon pick no cotton." She would tell me, "Rosie Mae, go get that sack and get in that field or I'm gon whip you." That's what she be telling me. And I tell her, "I ain't gon do nothing." And she say, "You will do it, you little young lady!" And so when I act like I be slowing down, she'll get a switch and start whipping me. And I'd go to hollering.

— Do you consider your family poor?

Uh-huh. Yeah, they poor. My father don't work now. He used to work at the peanut mill; he picked a little cotton sometime. He had a stroke in '64, I think. They get a check from security. I get a check for Michelle. I think I get seventy dollars a month. My brothers here, they sawmill.

— Where do you get your water?

We get our water up to that house up the road. Sometimes, have to tote it that far. Uh-huh, I've thought about I wished I had a faucet or something or other to run in the house. I bathe in a foot-tub. Every night. You're supposed to take a bath to keep from smelling.

— What about toilet facilities?

We don't have nary'n one of them. We go to the, you know, bushes.

— How do you feel about that?

I feel we should have a closet or something like that outside.

We don't have no electricity.

Seven people live here. We got one room and a kitchen. Me and my baby sleep together, two brothers sleep together, and Mama and my little brother sleep together and my daddy sleeps on a little folding bed. We all sleep in one room. It's just a two-room house.

— Have you ever thought about living in a real nice house?

Yeah, I thought of having a house with bedrooms and living room and dining room and kitchen, something like that. It would have pretty flowers and things. I have thought about it, but I don't know whether I will, though.

— When you were little did you get a lot of Christmas presents?

No, no more than Daddy tell Santa Claus to come to us. Tell Santa Claus to bring us things like dolls, tricycles, orange and apples and things. See, my daddy would go see Santa Claus, I'd tell him what I want.

I didn't get nothing one Christmas when I was little. I was about eleven. Because my daddy, he didn't have nothing to buy me nothing with. I told him I wanted some dresses and some dolls. He said he would of went to see Santa

Claus, but he didn't have no money to go. I didn't say nothing then. On Christmas, I felt kind of awful.

I haven't got nary'n a Christmas present since I was 'bout twelve, thirteen, something like that. I can't even hardly remember, it's been so long. My little brother don't get any neither. On Christmas, we cook some cakes, barbecue some chicken, make some salad, and make some pies.

— Do you give Christmas presents?

I gave Michelle and my mother something for Christmas last Christmas. I got Michelle some pants and two dresses and caps and shoes and socks. I got my mother a hat.

— Have you ever thought about why you are poor?

Uh-huh. Uh-huh, I've thought about it often.

— What goes through your mind when you think about it?

I think about I wished I had a lot of money and things like that.

— Do you ever think about why you are poor?

Uh-huh.

— What reasons have you thought of?

That question kind of got me kind of puzzled.

— Why do you think most whites are well-to-do while you are poor?

Because white peoples, they been having all their days and they'll make colored peoples get out in the field and work, but it ain't thataway now. It's better now. Colored peoples can have just like they have now. Some of 'em.

— Do you believe anyone powerful cares about poor people?

I don't know. I don't think so.

— What about the government?

Lester Maddox? He helps the poor people. He gives 'em commodities and he gives 'em checks and things like that. Yeah, I like him all right. I don't know anything about him, but that he's a good man.

•   •   •

They always say that rich peoples don't go to heaven, they go to the torment. That's what I've heard my mother say. She just say that rich people go to torment and poor people go to heaven, that's what she say.

— Have you ever looked at a rich person and said to yourself that when he dies he's going to torment?

Uh-huh. A lot of people. Mr. John Greer's one. He's white, yeah. He kills things, dogs and cats and things. He's killed two dogs and a cat of mine. About two years ago, he hauled off and killed them. The dogs was coming up a dirt

road and Mr. Greer was walking along there and he shot 'em. I saw him. I said, "He the one that got to pay for it, not me; he have bad luck." And he had bad luck. Lightning shocked him.

•   •   •

No, I never been to the dentist. I need to go though, because sometimes, for a long time, my teeth ache, be hurting.

•   •   •

No, I ain't never been to nary'n a movie. And we don't have a TV, ain't never had one.

•   •   •

I said one time that I wanted to go back to school. It been about a year after I had my baby, and I still do. I wanted to go back a heap, to learn some more. I said I was going to go back, but I just didn't go back. Because Mama said she wouldn't want to keep the baby. She said, "I can't keep her, because sometimes I don't feel like keeping her."

— Do you think an education is a good thing to have?

Uh-huh. Because if you don't have education, people be talking about you dumb and all of that. I think they talk about me like that.

— Which school were you thinking about going back to?

To the white. I just wanted to go back. I liked it all right.

— Even though they called you a nigger?

I called 'em a honky back.

•   •   •

You can't hardly find no job around here. If you find one they won't be paying you nothing all that much. Most of 'em work in the field around here. Work in the field. And in these parts they work you for nothing. Been working colored people for nothing all their days.

— Do you want to leave here?

I've just wanted to leave here because I'm tired of around here. Go somewhere where I can have a nice time. You have a nicer time up there than you do down here. You be going places, having a nice time.

— Have you thought about leaving lately?

Yeah. Been thinking about it about three or four months. I say, "Mama, I wish I could go to Hartford, live where my other sisters are, try to get me a job." She say, "You could go if you call your sister."

— Why haven't you called?

I just ain't called. I'm gon call. Might call next week. I'd tell her to send at me, me and my baby, and go up there and get me a job.

— What type of job would you try to get?

Something like working in a hospital. Like cleaning up, doing like that.

— [A couple of weeks later:] Is there anything you want to achieve in life?

I said one time I wanted to be a nurse. [Giggles.]

— You said you wanted to do cleaning work in a hospital; why did you change?

I just said that. I'd rather be a nurse; that's what I used to say when I was little. Teachers was asking us what we wanted to be when we grow up and I told 'em I wanted to be a nurse.

— Would you like to be able to attend a training school to learn to become a nurse's aide or operating room technician or something like that?

Yeah, I'd like that. [Giggles.] I'd really like that.

— Do you think you will ever go to Hartford and get a job in a hospital?

I think so, I don't know.

— Where do you think you will be living and what do you think you will be doing five years from now?

I might be dead in that time.

•   •   •

— When did you first learn about the difference between the status of colored and white people?

Since I got a little bigger. Oh, about sixteen. I just sat down one day and went to thinking. I was sitting down one day thinking about Gladys — that girl what I told you I liked at the white school — thinking she wasn't no more than colored people.

— But when did you first learn that whites think they're better?

Oh, I found that out when colored and white started going to school together.

— When you were a little kid, did your mother ever tell you that you couldn't go in certain places?

Yeah, she have told me that. Like the drugstore. Most the white children, they go in there; sometimes they have books in there and they be looking at 'em and reading 'em, and she'll tell us not to do it. I didn't say nothing, just walk along. I just wondered why I can't do it.

— Did you ever have any white playmates?

I had one white girl I used to play with when I was little, named Doris Daniel. We mostly played basketball and rolled on the grass. I didn't like her so hot when me and her played together. Sometimes she tell me to come down there and play with her, and she be wanting to jump on me, I'll go back home.

— Have you ever been insulted by white children; have they ever said bad things about you?

Uh-huh, at school. Sometimes we be sitting around to the lunchroom table, they call me ole nigger and I called 'em a honky back. I called 'em a honky.

— What about when you were a little girl?

When they called me a nigger then, I didn't say nothing. Like this white girl named Jean, sometimes she come by my house riding horses. She'd ride by and say, "Hey, ole nigger." And I wouldn't say nothing.

— How did you feel?

Call her cracker. I'd say to myself, "Ole cracker, calling me ole nigger."

— Were you ever jealous of white kids when you were little?

Huh-uh.

— Were you ever jealous of them for having nicer things than you had?

I'm Somebody Important

Uh-huh. After you see they have on them nice things, I just say I wish I could have some of those. I say it to myself.

— Do you still?

Yeah. Say it all the time. Like Mr. Cecil, he live down there on the river. I'd like to have his car and some money, that's all. He come by here a lot. He's got a light blue car. I'd like to have that. Because it's real pretty.

— How do you feel toward him when you see him drive by, good or bad?

Sort of bad. I don't know why.

— How do you feel toward most whites?

Lemme see. Some of 'em's all right. I hate some of 'em. I hate Mrs. Ruth Barnes . . . I hate a lot of 'em. Some white people look at you real mean, roll their eyes at you.

— What goes through your head when they do that?

Going through my head that they kind of hate me.

— Tell me about some of the white people you hate.

I hate a lady named Mrs. Edna. She Mr. Bob Smith's wife, they run a store over there. She calls colored peoples niggers. Like when little children be going to ice cream box to get some ice cream, she'll tell 'em, "Get out of there, ole nigger, I can get it myself."

And I hate a white lady named Mrs. Ruth Barnes. When we were staying on her place last year she used to say, "Get out of my yard, ole nigger." I'd call her ole honky. She wouldn't say nothing but look at me and roll her eyes then.

— Are there any white people you like?

I like Miss Nora Mercer. She treats colored people all right. She run a store. She just treat colored people nice. Some white peoples, you go to the store, they won't let you go in the boxes and things, but she would.

— Do you act any differently around white people than you do around colored people?

Uh-huh. Act more ashamed. Act kind of shy-like.

— Are you afraid of white people around here?

I used to be but I ain't now. I used to be scared that I'll whip 'em and then they might run back and tell their mama and daddy about it, come jump on me. I'll be scared.

Yeah, my parents are scared of white people. I think older people are more. Because every time a white man comes to older people's houses, they'll say, "Yes sir? No sir?" I think they be scared, saying *yes sir* and *no sir*. I think they should not say that. They ain't no more than us, no more than our skin is darker, they's is white.

— Do you say *yes sir* and *no sir* to whites?

Uh-huh, sometimes. But not usually.

— What is the worst thing that white people do to colored people?

Work 'em hard for nothing, that's all.

— How do you feel about them doing that?

I feel that colored people shouldn't work for 'em. I feel they should not work for 'em hardly for nothing, and they be getting all the benefit. I feel that anybody should have a good living.

— What changes would you like to see in the majority of whites?

I just think the whites, they should mix, because they ain't no better. I'd like to see 'em mix, that's all. There's a restaurant for the whites in Shady Grove. Because they think theirself better or something.

•   •   •

Huh-uh, I don't know what that means [prejudice].

Huh-uh, I never heard that word [integration].

Huh-uh, I never heard that word [discrimination].

Huh-uh, I've never heard of those [NAACP and SCLC].

Yeah, I've heard of the Black Panthers. They do a whole lot of fighting. I watch 'em on the news up at my sister's house. I think they all right. If you get 'em started up, they probably start killing; some of them will get killed though.

Yeah, I have heard about Martin Luther King. He's for the colored, that's all I know. I heard about him getting killed on television. I was up at this man and lady's house looking at TV. Cowboy picture was playing and it cut off and they said he got shot in the neck, and after then they said he died. I felt bad.

•   •   •

— Do you think the race situation has changed any during the past five years?

Yeah, I think it has changed some. Talking about white and colored? They're mixing, going to school together. It got better than it used to be.

— Do you think it will ever come to pass that white and colored will live side by side, treat each other right, and both have good jobs?

Yeah, I think so, I don't know. It might not be much longer. It might be about five years from now, I don't know.

— How do you think it will happen?

I don't know.

— Do you think it will just get that way or will people have to do things to make it that way?

Think people just have to do things to make it that way.

— Who's keeping it from coming about?

Might be some of the white peoples, I guess.

— Do you think they will change on their own?

Huh-uh. Probably have to get somebody to stop 'em. Demonstrators, I guess.

— If there were a demonstration here about something, would you join?

Uh-huh.

— Are you sure?

I'm sure I would. I think about it a lot of times.

— Why would you join one?

I would just like it. I would like it real good if it was to be around here. Sometimes I just get thinking about it. To just straighten out some of these people through here, I'd like it. It just make me feel good and I be glad of it.

— Do you think the white people around here would like it?

No, they wouldn't hardly like it.

— What if you were demonstrating and some white people came by and said, "Nigger, I'm going to bust your head."

I think I would bust theirs back.

— Do you think it's important to vote?

Uh-huh. I registered to vote Saturday before last. Mrs. Kendrick took me. Like if you don't have no way to go, she'll take you. She came by here and said she wanted to take me.

— Say a colored man and Lester Maddox were running for governor, which would you vote for?

The colored. I'd just vote for him, I don't know why.

•   •   •

— What do you daydream about?

Daydream? Talking about just sit up and look? I know I have daydreams . . . a lot. Lemme see what I daydream about. Sometimes I daydream about Michelle and sometimes about myself. Dream about I'm eating. I'm eating. I be gnawing. On some peas and cornbread and drinking milk.

•   •   •

— When were you the scardest?

Like when somebody die.

— Why does that make you scared?

Because I be scared they'll come around and haint me.

— Who's died that you were afraid would haint you?

My uncle and my little brother. I thought my little brother would come back and haint me. It worried me a lot. He didn't come back and haint me though.

But I have seen one dead person. Man what got kilt back up there, he got stabbed. A man named Tommy Hill stabbed him in the chest. I think they were playing cards, and he didn't want to give him some money, so he stabbed him. And the next day after they buried him, I seed him. It like to scared me to death.

I seed him, he come to our back door. I was so scared. He was looking just like he was natural though. He come through the house. See, both of the doors was open. The house had kind of a hall between it, and he come in the front door and went on out the back door. I saw him. It looked like every strand of my hair was sticking up on my head. I felt a heartbeat. My older brother, Charlie, seen him too. I was so scared I just couldn't do nothing. Just stand there and holler. I just said, "Oooooh, Mama!" See, we just knowed this man real well. See, he was kind of crazy about us. He would send us to the store a lot. He would send us to the store to get something for him and give us money for going.

My uncle didn't haint me. But my brother saw him one morning before day. My uncle wouldn't let him make the fire in the stove and so my brother reached up to pull on the light and my uncle looked right in his face.

•   •   •

— What are your happiest childhood memories?

Well, when I go to a party when I was little I was happy to go. Like a birthday party. I remember a real happy one when Mama gave herself a birthday party. I was happy then. We just had a nice time. Her sister, her brothers, and aunts and things came. We danced and eat.

— Have you ever had a birthday party?

No. I think it would be nice if I was to have one.

— Will you ever give Michelle a party?

Yeah, I probably will. This August I'll invite her cousin and a lot of peoples, and her uncles and Catherine, George, and Betty and that's about all. I told my cousin I'm gon give Michelle a birthday party. I'm gon get her three dresses and some shoes and socks and some bows.

•   •   •

My two brothers been in trouble before. They had a pistol one time and, you know, they sent 'em off to something sort of like a reformatory school. They say they had a pistol, I don't know. They sent 'em off. They didn't find a gun, they just come and got 'em and put 'em in jail. See, this boy's grandmother issued out a warrant for 'em. Michael Moore's grandmother. See, he come back and told her they had a gun.

— How did you feel when they were sent away?

I felt bad because I believe they didn't do that, didn't shoot at him. Police said they shot at Michael Moore. They was in there about eight or nine months. I went to crying, I missed 'em. I don't believe they did it.

•   •   •

— What's the most exciting thing that ever happened to you?

Nothing, I don't guess.

◦   •   •

— If you could have three wishes that would come true, what would they be?

I would wish I could go to Hartford, that would be my first wish. That's about all I would wish.

•   •   •

— Is there any dream you keep having at night?

I dream about sometimes I find money. I find the money in a stump and I run to — I don't know the lady — I run to her, she take it away from me. And sometimes I dream about Michelle's father, he be giving me some money.

•   •   •

— When are you sad?

Sad when somebody die. I'll be sad then. I get sad when anybody die. Even if I don't know 'em very well, I still be sad. I just will get sad time I hear it. I stay sad a good while, until they bury 'em.

•   •   •

— When do you feel the most alive?

Dancing, I feel all right.

•   •   •

The worst thing ever happened to me? Well, when I was little I fell and cut my leg on a piece of tin, that was bad. I couldn't walk about two or three

months. I was about seven or eight. I went a week before I went to the doctor. You could see the bone. The doctor said you should of done brought her before. He just gave me two shots and some pills, and put some powder on it, and bandaged it up. He said it'd gone too long to put stitches in it. It hurt me sometimes now.

•　•　•

A lady that stays right down the road, she named Mrs. Dorothy Phillips, she real mean. Every time she come up here she be whipping on my baby, she be whipping on Michelle. She whip her with a strap. Because Michelle come up to her and she go whipping.

— What do you say to her?

I tell her don't whip my baby no more.

— Have you ever hit this woman?

I have sassed her . . .

•　•　•

My biggest hope is I'll get a car and that one day I'll get rich or something like that.

— Do you think you will?

That's what I hope.

•　•　•

— What are you most afraid of?

I'm kind of afraid to die. I just say I wish I wouldn't never die.

— Do you think about that very often?

Yeah, everybody should think about dying.

•　•　•

— [Junior, Michelle's father, came home to Shady Grove for the first time in two years near the end of our interview sessions.] What happened when Junior came?

He just come and gave me some money, thirty-five dollars, for Michelle; I kissed him.

— You said you were going to hit him.

I said I was gon hit him, but I didn't. I was glad to see him. I said, "Hey, Yokie, darling." They call him Yokie. He said, "Hey, honey sugar pie and darling."

— Was this the first time he'd seen Michelle?

Yeah.

— What did he say about her?

He just said, "I'm glad to see my baby." He just went to kissing her and went to playing with her. She act like she got scared of him.

— What did you all talk about?

I just asked him about how come he went off and stayed so long. He just said reason he hadn't come back was because he was working or something or nuther, couldn't hardly get no vacation. He be living in Miami, he said.

— Did you still feel mad at him?

Huh-uh. I just said that before. He come Friday, left Monday. And we went up there to the juke up there every day together.

— How did you feel when he left?

I didn't care when he left because I was mad with him. Because I was like I was. About how he had messed me up. And then I started getting mad with him.

— When did you start feeling mad again?

I didn't feel mad with him, not till I was with the baby.

— Did you ask him to stay?

He fixing to come back next month. I said, "Yokie, you gon stay this time?" He said huh-uh, he was coming back next month.

— What would you think if he asked you to marry him and move away with him?

I think all right about it. I'd do it because I love him.

•   •   •

The proudest I ever been? Like when you get proud on something? I was real proud when I had Michelle, I was proud. And I was proud when I was getting her. I was proud then.

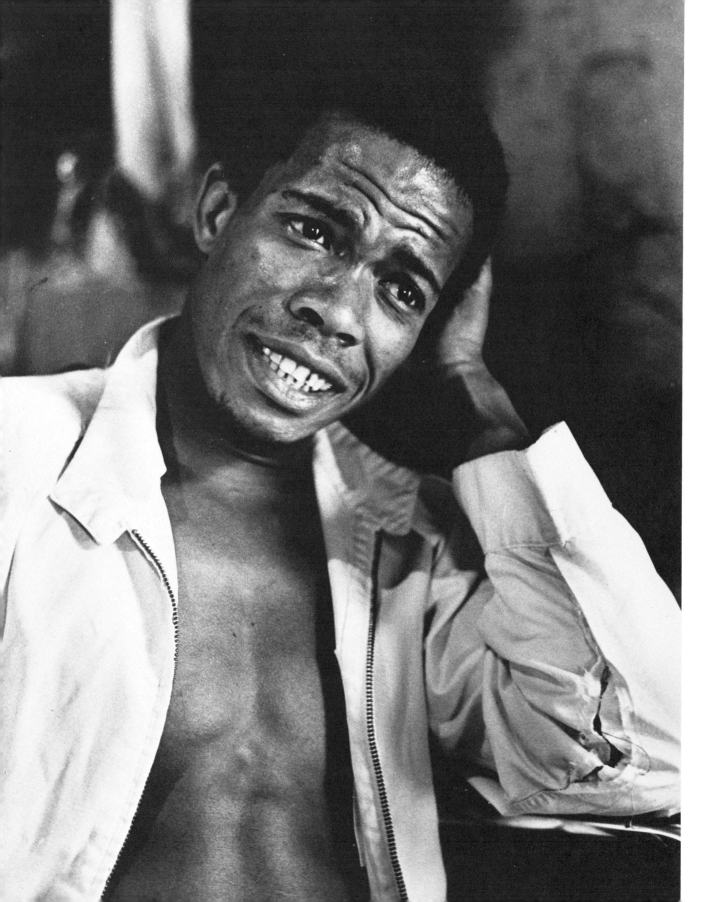

Bobby Gaines

Most of his life Bobby Gaines has lived alone with his grandmother in Baxter, Georgia, but his father and his father's family now stay with them. Bobby is twenty-two years old, but he just graduated from high school. He seems to pride himself on his ability to discourse on any subject. When he thought he was especially qualified to answer some question during the interviews, he would light a cigarette, take off his sunglasses, lean back in his chair, and begin with "Well, George . . ." He chose his words carefully and usually pronounced them precisely.

I would say the thing that stuck in my mind most as a little kid was the day the cops came and got me. I was very young — about two years old, maybe three — and that stuck. That's a long story but I'll try to narrow it. Oh, I guess you would call it a conflict between my mother and father. So they got a divorce and they was trying to decide on who was going to be my, you know — how should I say it? — well, they was trying to decide who would get me, my mother or my father. My mother wanted me to stay with her mother and my father wanted me to stay with him.

But the lawyer had made it clear that I was to go to my father, you know. And my mother didn't know about it, they hadn't told her yet because it had happened about the day before then. I was with my mother, and my father got the police so there wouldn't be any conflict, I guess. Because, you know, naturally a mother isn't gon give her kid up. So he got the cops to come over with him, so there wouldn't be any mess. And he got me and brought me back over here.

And what happened I don't know, but it ended up I was living with my grandmother, my father's mother. And I been with her ever since, barring the exception of going down to Palm Beach, Florida, to see Mama on holidays and during the summer — she gotten married again and she got five kids. And I would say up until about seven years ago, just my grandmother and I was living together; she raised me all the way up from a little child to today.

I guess it was about '62 or '63 that my father, his wife, and their five kids moved in here. So you got nine people living here, with the kids.

— How did you feel when they moved in here?

Well, actually, I didn't see anything wrong with it. He didn't have, you know, a solid education, so he couldn't get a good job. He's a pulpwood worker. And they needed a place to stay and whereas he was working, he was making enough to buy food and clothes and pay small bills. So here he didn't have to pay any rent or anything. And I go along with it.

•   •   •

— Do you get along better with your mother or father?

Mother. Between my father and myself there seems to have been a few links missing. He went to the Army and he wasn't around me too much and I just grew up without him around. And something seem to have went haywire during this time and we just don't communicate.

— Do you ever argue or get in fights?

No, heck no. We just don't communicate much. Say he come in, he would say, "Hello." I'd say, "Hi" or "Good afternoon." Or sometime he ask me, "Do you have a match or a cigarette or something?" We communicate, but I wouldn't say as strong as a father and a son should.

— Can you communicate pretty well with your mother?

Uh-huh. Even though she had five kids since she had me, she said I'm still the baby. As big as I am, I'm still the baby. If I say, "Mama, I want this or I want that," just like my grandmother — "Okay." Just as simple as that — "Okay."

— Are you closer to your mother or grandmother?

Grandmother. Way closer, because you know I've spent my life around here, and she's bought me clothes to go on my back when I was a kid, and she put food in my mouth when I was a kid, and she's sort of taken the place of mother, you know, at home.

How do I feel about her? I love her, I'll do anything I can for her. As soon as I get some of the things in life that I've wanted, I want her to share them.

— What are the good points and the bad points of your grandmother?

Good points and bad points? Believe it or not, so far I've seen no bad points. She's a very nice lady. All the neighbors like her, and maybe they're going to the supermarket, they'll come by, stop, and talk for an hour or more. I haven't seen any bad points.

— What about your mother?

My mother? The bad points, she's got a temper like I have. And she'll clobber one of the kids with maybe a broom. They do something wrong, she'll grab her broom and maybe slap them on the butt. Good points, she's got a good heart, she's thoughtful, she loves her kids, she loves her family, and just like my grandmother, any other good quality that you could think of that a person should have, she's got it.

— And your father?

Bad points? I don't believe in a lot of things he do, like getting stoned and using profanity. He drinks too heavy.

— What's he like when he's drunk?

A madman.

— Tell me about some of the things he does.

A madman — ha, ha — that's pretty good. Well, have a scrap with his old lady. *Every time* he get drunk.

— Does he hit her?

Does he?! Pretty good.

— So what are his other bad points and good points?

Bad points . . . He got that temper too. I think that's why I'm messed up; you know, that's why I got a firecracker temper. My mother, she got a pretty good temper, my father has too, so I got to have something. And that's about the only bad points I can see. But when he's sober, he's an entirely different person. He's the spitting image of his mother when he's sober. He's got all those good qualities.

•   •   •

Both my grandmother's legs had to come off. When we moved over here to this house in '62, I think she stepped on a tack. She didn't think it was anything serious, but the thing was in her shoe and she didn't know it and it kept working up and working up until it pierced her foot. And through piercing her foot, it blood-poisoned her, and so they had to take one of her legs off. And in '65,

Bobby Gaines   201

I believe it was, the other leg came off. This time she was burning some trash in the back, and she had some clothes on the line and the wind was blowing and it blew a sheet off. And she tried to catch it and by doing this she stepped in some of this fire and it got in her shoe . . . And she's a diabetic and so this burnt her. She didn't think it was too bad so she didn't go to the doctor, I think she put some of this pain-killer stuff on it. It kept the pain off all right, but the thing got infected. So they had to take her other leg off.

Before that, she was a cook in a restaurant, and very good at that. But she had to stop working. And when she stopped, I started. After what happened, I had to sort of go for myself. I would work to buy my clothes, pay for my lunch at school, and just, you know, buy small necessities. The rest we got from her disability check.

She had always given me a good life; I've never had to worry about anything, clothes or . . . But since I've gotten to be a pretty good-sized boy I do that myself, because I revere my clothes. That's one of my hobbies — buying clothes. I like 'em, you know. I like to go neat. And I like to wear clothes that look good. It's true that clothes doesn't make the person alone, but it helps a heck of a lot. And I know a lot of people judge you by your appearance, which I think is a mistake — not a total mistake, but a slight mistake. So therefore I kept my mind sharp, kept my body sharp.

• • •

— Was your grandmother pretty strict when you were a child?

Oh, she was about as strict on me as maybe any grandmother would be to a kid.

— How strict was that?

Oh, strict enough to tear my butt up when I did something wrong.

— Did she do that very often?

No, because during the time that I was growing up I was a pretty good kid. I didn't get into many fights, but there was one that I never will forget. When just my grandmother and I were living together, my grandmother and a neighbor was just real tight girlfriends. And this neighbor, she had a boy that was about a year younger than I was — he was about eleven — and he was a little smaller than me, but he could beat my butt. *Every day* we would get into it, you know, about a tricycle or a cap pistol or something.

And one Sunday we started fighting over a small bike and I ran home. I ran in the house, I was crying. My grandmother said, "What's wrong?" I told her about it. She said, "Let me tell you something. You're too big to run; stand up and fight." She said, "Next time he fight you, if you don't stand up and fight,

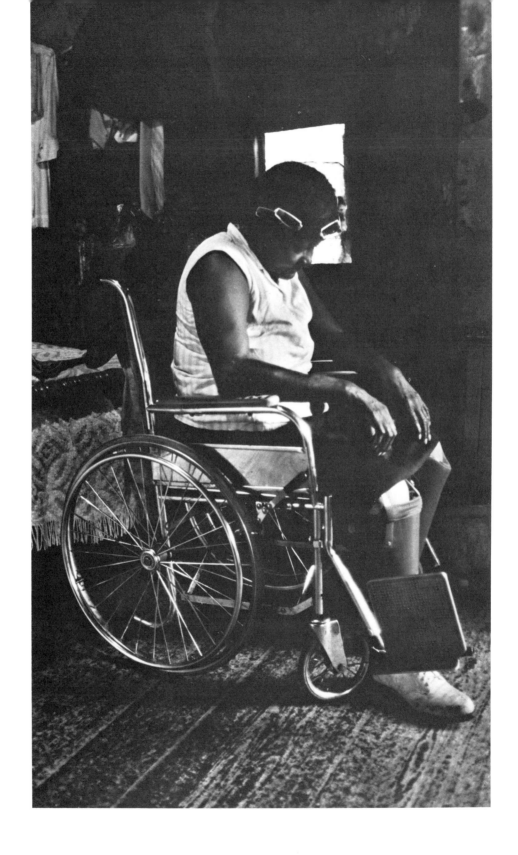

when you come home we're gon fight. I'm gon tear your butt up." She went and got a long switch to prove it. I said, "God-dog, I know I got to do something or I'll get two whippings — one from him and one from her."

And that afternoon, me and that boy was down to a friend's house, and I said something and he said, "You shut up." I said, "Well, you don't tell me what to do." And he said, "You better shut up, I'll beat your butt." And I said, "No, you won't either." He said, "I will." I said, "No you won't." He said, "Step off the porch then."

I stepped off the porch and as soon as I stepped on the ground, he caught me — whop! — on side of the head. And I staggered back. And, you know, all his friends were sitting on the porch and they said, "Oh, oh, Henry is about to beat Bobby." So I said, "No he's not." And we tied up. And I was eating him up. And I think that's when I first started swinging these big fists.

— Have you gotten in many fights since then?

Not too many. Since then, the guys, they know that I'm pretty strong. They know if I make contact with my fists, that's it. And I don't bother anybody and don't anyone bother me, so I haven't gotten in many fights. But I've got to say I've gotten in a few.

One started over a girl at this hangout, where all the fellows and girls hang out at this café. One night last year our crowd was around and we was drinking beer and feeling pretty good. And I was going with this girl, and this guy that wasn't even with the crowd, he came up, started bull-jiving: "I'll take Bobby's girl," you know, "I'll take Barbara," you know. "Bobby doesn't have a tight hold on her. He doesn't know what to do for her," and all that stuff.

And I said, "Cool it, man. Look, don't drag my name in the dirt. Don't take me down, dog, give me a break with my girl."

"No, I'm gon take that girl with me."

I said, "Okay, you go on and take her then." And I thought about it, you know, and I said, "Heck, he can't take anything from me. He's just making me mad," you know. And that's when that firecracker shot up on me, you know, that temper. And so I caught him up side the head and he caught the ground. And I started for him, he got up and took off. It wasn't a fight, you know. It sort of a "I-hit-you, you-hit-the-ground."

— You say that firecracker temper . . .

I can control it, but . . . I have to because, you know, I tell the fellows, I say, "Look, don't bug me because I got a temper as hot as the hottest day in September," you know. I do have a pretty hot temper, but thank God I can control it.

. . . Oh, I forgot — prom night I got into a fight. And that was a time I couldn't walk off. Usually, see, I walk off, because when I get mad enough to fight, I be too mad to fight, really. Because I'll pick up something and hurt somebody, and so instead of just hurting a man and feeling bad afterward, I just walk off. If he'll let me. But if he doesn't let me walk off, then we'll have to lock heads.

So prom night I got into one. For the setting of the prom there was a pool of water in the middle of the floor and there was this fountain that's skeeting the water up and this pool was catching the water and there was water in the pool. And maybe about five minutes to one, just before it was over, I walked by the pool. And this guy was splashing all in the water, man, you know, like he was cracking up — just splashing, new shoes, new suit . . . I think we rented tuxedoes . . . But, no, he had on a brown suit. And I had on a tuxedo — clean, decked down. I walked by the pool and he stepped out of the pool, and while he was stepping out he kicked some water up and the water splashed all over me. We're cousins and so I thought it was an accident, you know, and I stopped and brushed the water off of me. I thought he was gon say, you know, "I'm sorry, excuse me, I apologize." But he didn't say anything. He looked back at me and gave me that — he was drunk really — he gave me that look like "Go to hell, man." I said, "Good God!" That's when that temper did just like that, it was gone.

And I went over and pushed him and he fell over about five or six chairs. And I turned around to walk off and he ran behind me and grabbed me from behind. And I said, "God-dog, I'm messed up now — my tuxedo and everything — I'll never do this again, you know, go to a prom and everything." And he slung me down. And I grabbed his head because I didn't want to hurt him. I just held his head and really I tried to break his neck because I was that mad. And the next thing I knew, the principal was pulling me off. And I said, "Turn me loose." You know, I didn't know who had me. And I looked back and saw it was him and he said, "Cool it, Bobby. Don't do this, this is wrong." I said, "I know it, but this guy, he got to show me some respect." So he said, "I'll see about it Monday." I said, "No you won't see about it Monday, because I'm gon kill this punk." And he pulled me back and my girl, she had been over on the side crying and telling me, "Bobby, stop, stop, stop." But I was too mad. When I get angry I just get uncontrollable.

•   •   •

The reason I'm twenty-two and just got finished school, that's a long story, but I'll tell it to you if you really want to hear it . . . From the first to the ninth grade, school had always been my thing; crazy about it. But when I got in the ninth grade I started tipping around with girls, you know, and a lot of guys had quit and were working and I said, "Heck, look like those fellows are having more fun than the ones in school is." I said, "Heck, I'm gon quit." Quit.

— What did your grandmother say?

She started to kill me, that's how she felt. "What are you quitting for?"

"I'm just tired of school."

"Well, Bobby, you're old enough to know you're wrong and if that's what you want to do, *you do it* and I want you to learn the hard way that you are making a big mistake."

And, brother, believe me, I learned. Tried to get a job; I think I got one for a little while, very short time, wasn't interesting . . . And then I just gave it up and didn't do anything and, man, that's what I don't understand. What the heck! — I guess I was just trying to do like the boys. I just shot pool, hussled pool, stayed around home, and walked the streets.

— Did you do nothing the whole time you were out of school?

Well, no . . . If I have to tell you about everything I did, you're opening up an old scar.

— I'd like to hear about it if you wouldn't mind telling me about it.

Well, it's really dipping in the past. I didn't want to mention it, but those years mostly I was in this juvenile or training school or whatever you want to call it. I got sent there twice, I believe it was. I started associating with those boys that were having fun, you know, and I found out they was burglarizing. So the first time I got sent I believe it was for burglary.

So one of my rap partners and I, we wanted to make some quick money. What for, I still don't know! And why did we do it, I still don't know! But we went in this place and didn't expect this person to come back, but she did and she walked in on us. Man, shit, my heart jumped in my mouth! She came back and caught us and, man, I dived through the bottom of the window and he went through the top; the whole window came out, everything. So we ran — I think that's why I'm so doggone strong in my legs now — I ran for about five miles, I believe, not knowing where I'm going, just in a circle, just running scared.

So, some type of way they found out who we was and they got us and they put me under parole and I broke the thing. They told me, "Stay at home, go to school every day." But I didn't go back every day and I didn't stay at home. So the man wrote me a letter and said meet him at the courthouse. I met him. He dropped the hammer on me and that was it.

I'm Somebody Important   206

— How did you feel about being sent to reform school?

I didn't give a heck. I said, "Well, heck, I lost out on life now, so the heck with it." I didn't care about too many things. You've seen some people that don't give a doggone about anything, don't do anything, and that's the way I felt.

— How did your grandmother feel when you were being sent to reform school?

She hated it. She would just show that it, you know, hurt her, in facial expressions. You know, she wouldn't just come right out and say it, but I could tell from facial expressions that it hurt her and from the way she talked.

— How old were you, about fifteen?

Somewhere in that area. But really to go back and say exactly, this is something I've forgotten; going there was something I had put out of my mind, you know. And to go back and give detail for detail, I can't if my life depended on it. If someone had a .38 cocked on me I couldn't go in all the details about it.

But being in there gave me a lot of experience, I learned about a lot of people. And *that* is where I developed a little pure hate for whites. The guards, they're animals.

— The guards were white?

Uh-huh. Oh . . . they integrated the guards during the time I was there. They kept the guys segregated, had all white on one side and all black on one side, but when I was there they got some black guards, too, for the black side. They were asses. White and black.

They're not allowed to beat you in there, but they'd get those guys and beat the heck out of them! I know the fellows would aggravate them some, but they would hit a kid when it wasn't necessary. And one hit me once, you know, and I couldn't hold it back, man, I tore his head up. I tried to bust his head open.

I was brushing my teeth and one of the fellows came by and hit me on the back, you know, and I swallowed some of that stuff, toothpaste. So I said, "Goddurn it" — I've never cursed, that's one thing about me, there's not an elderly person around here that can say they heard me use profanity, but around the guys I do pretty good. And I said, "Goddurn it," and I grabbed him; you know, just kidding.

So this white guard, he said, "What did you say? Didn't you say goddamn it?" I went out there, I said, "No sir, I didn't. I said goddurn it." And the guy that I pushed on, he told him, he said, "No sir, Bobby just said goddurn it, because I hit him in the back."

"You know you don't curse around me like that, you respect me!" I said, "I didn't say that."

"You calling me a liar?" I said, "No sir, I'm not calling you a liar."

Bap! He slapped me. And then this colored guard, he ran over there like he was gon hit me too, and he said, "Who you cussing, who you puffing up at?" I said, "Nobody." He said, "Boy, don't you know I'll tear your head up?" I said, "Yes sir." He said, "I ought to beat your ass anyway."

So then I got steamed up, you know, and I got a hot temper. I stood up and I said, "No you will not," and the white guard ran over. "You know you don't talk to a guard like that." I said, "I'll tell you the same thing — you *will not* beat me. I'll go to the superintendent, I'll tell the board, the governor, and anybody else if you beat me. I'm gon tell them about it if you don't kill me. You'd better kill me."

So he hit me again, the white guard did, and when he hit me I slapped him. And the colored guard, he came over and he hit me with his fist and so I shot him up side of the head with my fist. So they tore my butt up. They got a big board and told me to stoop over, and I had to because they had called over the intercom and sent for more guards. And so he laid it on my butt. But I told him when he got through, I said, "If you ever let me see you in the streets I'll make you remember this."

They don't seem to accept the fact that if a young man make a mistake, they're there to coach him, you know, guide him along, help him out, show him that he was wrong and if he want to correct himself, they're there to help him. I think that's what they're there for. And I think the governor thinks that's what they're there for, to coach the young people. Whereas they don't coach them, a lot of fellows, they make them meaner. Whereas me, I say thank God I was fortunate. I didn't hold it in my heart for them. I came out and started thinking about Bobby's life. See, this thing with the guards happened the second time I was in there.

When I got out the first time, I was too ashamed to go back to school. I was too ashamed to face a lot of people and along with that no-caring mood I was just in a heck of a mess; a mellovahess, I'll put it that way — that's the principal's word. So I continued to goof off. And I goofed up on it again.

And that time, you know, I said, "Heck, I goofed up too much," and after the experience I had there with the guards and being around some of the people, it sort of awakened me. There was a man there, I never will forget him. Green, the counselor, he told me, he said, "Bobby, you got good qualities. The thing about this place, I don't understand why people like you are here, you don't need to be here. You're not the type of person to have a life of crime, a bad life rather." So we talked and we talked. And he kept counseling and counseling and counseling. And he started me looking at things at a different point of view. I think that's when some of that meanness and hatred started vanishing.

So I got out that time, and being in there, it pushed me. A lot of people were saying that "he not gon be anything but a delinquent, a bum, a hoodlum, he's messing around with the wrong crowd and he's gon be just like they are." So I broke away from this crowd. I said I'm gon show the people that even though a man does make a mistake, don't brand him, give him a chance, you know. So I came back, went back to school, I put all effort forward and, man, I've been commended from that side of town to this side. By everybody really. You've got principals to superintendents, by a lot of local people . . . It makes you feel good, man, to know you made a J.A. out of somebody, you know. I sit back and laugh at it.

— Besides what you have already mentioned, what made you decide to go back to school?

I thought about it and I said I should go talk with the principal, because we've always been fond of one another. See, before he became principal he was a teacher and I was in his algebra class in the ninth grade and I was pretty good at it. And he recognized me for just a knack to want to learn even when I didn't know something. And he just admired me, he said he admire a curious young man.

So I went and talked with him. He told me, he said, "Bobby, whatever you get from life you'll put in life, or in other words, whatever life give you, you would have already given it." So I said, "Well, I'll think on it." He said, "I'll give you another thing to think over. When an individual does your thinking, they control you." And the thing that stayed in my mind was: Go back, go back; even though your classmates will be graduating, go back, you can make it. And I got it embedded in my head, I said I was gon get my education. I wanted to be somebody and I am — one day I will be.

— Were you nervous about going back?

Oh man, God-dog, I was real nervous, but they didn't know it and I didn't show it, you know. I knew people knew who I was and I knew what they was thinking. I said I know they not gon say anything to me about it because, you know, I had lifted weights for about a year and a half. And you would just look at me, you'd say, "Dog, he's a powerhouse, I know I'm not gon give him any junk." And I said I know they're not gon start anything or try to insult me, so the only thing I got to do is face the people. So I said to God to give me enough courage to face these people and I'll do the rest.

And, you know, a funny thing happened. Heck, when I went there I was nervous, but didn't anyone know it, I didn't show it. And would you believe in half a day I was walking around, peoples was walking up to me, a lot of people didn't know who I was: "Hello, who are you, are you a new boy, you just starting here, what's your name?" you know. And I started digging in my boots, I started carrying myself in a way as to where people would see that I wanted respect, that I was giving respect. And I made real good grades — this was junior year — and I did outstanding things in my class and for the school. So they — you know, the principal, the art teacher, his wife, and Miss Watson — saw that I was really trying, they saw that I was giving it all I had and they backed me up, gave me confidence.

This last term, my senior year, when I came back from Florida, the kids said, "Bobby, you want to run for class president?" And, man, that was a big honor, you know. I thought, "Me? The hoodlum, the bum? Me class president? The spokesman for the entire senior class?" I said, "You sure you want me?" They said, "Yeah, we believe that you know things about life, a few of the facts, you can talk to the principal and we believe that you have enough guts to stand up for us when we're not there." So I said, "Sure I'll run for class president." And this guy that I was running against, he had never dropped out of school, he was a honor student — which I was too last year, but he had been from the ninth grade — and he was well known. But would you believe that I beat him by forty-five or fifty votes, just went out of sight of him?

.   .   .

— Are you and the principal still close?

Uh-huh. After I dropped out and came back, we was even tighter. We was closer and he would advise me. He would tell me encouraging things to give me confidence. Like maybe I would go by and tell him. "Look, I want to go to college, but I'm afraid to, because maybe my past would throw a reflection on me." So he would say, "No. Don't look back, you're going forward. I don't think your past would have any type of bearing on your future in college or anywhere if you keep going the way you're going."

And I think that's true. I remember my last job. I had been working about three days before this man brought an application for me to fill out. I guess he thought I needed help filling it out, so he was helping me. And when we got to the part where it said had you ever been convicted of a felony, he said, "No, keep on going. Write 'no' all the way down there." You know, he could just tell by the way I carried myself that I hadn't been in anything. I liked that because it shows me that I could say to myself, "Boy, you've made a tremendous change."

.   .   .

— Did you go to school regularly after you went back?

Uh-huh, I fell in love with it. It was a challenge to me. Go in the class, the teacher would say, "What's so and so, who was the first governor of somewhere?" Someone would get up to answer and it would be wrong, you know, and I would come in and answer — that was a thrill, and I just fell in love with doing things like that. And now that I got my diploma, I hate to leave it. I got my diploma night before last.

I was so happy that night. I had to walk across the stage and the superintendent, he said, "Well, Prez, you made it." I said, "Yes sir." He said, "Bobby, I wish you the best of luck in the world." "Thank you sir." Went over there and shook the principal's hand and he said almost the same thing. "This is it, Prez." I said, "Yes sir." "God bless you, Bobby." I said, "God bless you." I was so happy. I felt as if I was sitting . . . where? On the very top of the world, looking down on everything that was beautiful. And I just felt happy, you know, because that was something I had been striving for and I finally gotten it. And everybody was shaking my hand and saying, "You've made an outstanding young man out of yourself."

— How did your grandmother feel when you got the diploma?

Well, she felt about like I did. She was happy, because she's always said, you know, before she died she wanted to see me graduate. She said that was one of the last things she wanted to see me do. So I did it. And you can imagine how happy she was.

•   •   •

— What do you like to do for fun?

Get me a good football game going, fish, hunt, play baseball . . . Oh, really about everything that the average healthy young man would like and could do. And I don't like anything better than getting me a good — not touch — but good hard tackle football game going. And on Friday and Saturday nights, that's when my girl comes in. If they're not having a dance we might go out to a café or something or we might go to her house and sit around and do a little of that good smooching.

— Do things ever get boring around here?

Very much so. But there's time when I like quietness, like to think. Sometime I'll go out in the yard and sit down for a couple of hours thinking. I like to think a lot.

— What do you think about?

Mostly my future and plans I have for it, and some thoughts go back to some of the crazy things I've done, some of them heck things that happened. Sometime the old lady cross my mind too, you know, my girl.

— What have you done during the past three summer vacations?

Oh boy, *those* are some things that I think about too. Went to Florida and stayed with my mother, worked, fished. Ah, man, that was a summer to remember. On the beach, this girl, she was a dreamboat, she was a junior in high school. Last year she was a junior and she owned her own car, she had a '69 Mustang, and she would come by and pick me up and we would go to the beach. We would go out on the beach and spread a blanket out, throw out a mountain of records and listen to records and eat chips and have colas and sometimes a little booze, and just have fun.

And my mother, she got a fabulous place. Beautiful, beautiful! They paid ten thousand dollars for it. And it has an upstairs and downstairs and it's extremely large. As a matter of fact, sometimes I get a taxi to bring me home from work when Mama can't make it or something. I'd tell him I want to go to 1837 Wyntton. He would get to where Mama live and keep on going straight down the road and he stopped. I said, "That's it right back there, man."

"You mean right back there?" I said, "Yeah." So he asked me about six or seven times, "You live here, this your house?" I kept on telling him. "Yeah, man, I live here."

"Dog, man, that's a mansion, you've got it made, what your daddy do, what your mommy do?" I said, "Brother, you getting too deep, getting too personal now."

— What does your mother's husband do?

He's a chef, bakes doughnuts.

·   ·   ·

— Do you remember the maddest you ever got?

The maddest I ever been was with a girl. As soon as I came back from juvenile, I started school and the principal, he told me, "You should put girls aside, but if you get one you get one that's intelligent and neat and nice and that's all around good." And so I got me one like that, you know, and we made it pretty good. But another guy came in the picture and so she gave me the heave-ho, you know. And I think I got pretty steamed up. Here I am trying to get back with her, and she stood there saying, "No, it won't work." See, I acted pretty nutty sometimes, you know. We could go to the café where the young people hang out, and we could be sitting around a table and I see some of the guys and, heck, I get up and start shooting the bull with the boys and forget she was there. And then I say, "God-dog it, I left my girl!" And then she would be gone and when I would see her again, she would fly off the handle. And so she said it wouldn't work to get back together and I'm trying to tell her, "Give me another break, give me another chance, let me prove myself." And she said, "No, it *won't* work."

— Out of the girls you've gone with, tell me about the one you cared most about.

One that I cared the most about? I think that was the one I've been talking about.

— Why?

Why? Because I couldn't get her like I wanted, I guess that's why. But the girl that I got now, I'm crazy about her.

— Tell me about the other one, the one that broke up with you.

Well, she was nice. I would go to her house, we would sit around, she would play records, and we would get close, you know, start a thing and we'd get excited and all that. But she always kept me back — you know, like whoa, man, that's far enough. She would always draw that line and when I got beyond that line she would maybe let me go a step beyond, but as far as going all the way across the line, nope. I guess that was something that made me think about her a lot. Plus the fact that I probably could have stayed with her, but as I said, I acted a nut. She said I neglected her. Which in a way I did, but I really didn't intend to.

— How did you feel when she put you down?

Felt terrible. I think I was sick for a week. Or maybe longer. Because you know I had a pretty strong feeling for this girl and we was in the same class and it's something when you got a feeling for a girl and you've broken up and you've got to sit in the same class with her. You might look up and accidentally catch her looking at you or you might look at her and she catch you looking at her. And I don't know, just get an awful feeling.

— Do most of the girls you go with let you go all the way across the line?

Most of the girls that I went with would let me go way across the line, yeah. At first, usually I would use the playboy approach. I wouldn't just do things straight out. When we was alone, you know, I would get close and I would get things set up. So when I did maybe pop a question, you know, or make that gesture, they would know what I'm referring to. And I would say I did a pretty good job.

The girl I go with now, her name is Joyce. She's a nice girl. She's thoughtful. She loves me. And I think I love her. I love her, I will say.

— Are you sure?

Oh, I wasn't sure, but we kind of broke up for a little while about three weeks ago and I found out then that I was sure. And some day, after we get what we want, we might get married.

— Have you talked about it?

We've talked about it, yeah. I had been thinking about not going to college or trade school or anything, just working, saving my money, and buy me a trailer. And we would get married. But we talked it over and she said, "Well, Bobby, it would be nice for you to go to school and come out and then after we get everything set up the way we want it, then we go into the details more closely." And I agreed.

— Why did you temporarily break up about three weeks ago?

Well, that's not too pleasant. She caught another girl sitting in my lap, another girl that she said I had been going with, you know. The way it happened, I think she was in typing class, and some friends went in and called her out and told her to come there, they had something to show her. And she came out and looked and I didn't see her, you know, and a bunch of guys were sitting around in the hall and one of 'em said, "Uh-oh, Red, you messed up." I said, "What do you mean 'messed up'?" You know, I just bull-jiving with the broad sitting on me. And one of the guys points and whispers, "Look, look, look." I looked around and saw my girl standing there and her eyes were about as big as a half a dollar. I think mine got as large as a silver dollar. And I couldn't think of anything to do but jump up. And so my girl gave me the devil about it. "I told you to stay away from her."

So we almost busted up after that, because, you know, I have a reputation of being quite a playboy, did everything sneaky. Before I started going with her, every girl that I saw that I liked, I would say, "Get that girl, man, she's fine, get her." But my girl didn't believe in that two and three and four and five stuff.

But back then, I did. Just for the heck of it, I wanted to see how far I could go last year, how many of 'em I could get. I would get a girl, just to see if I could get her, you know; it was a challenge to me. And after I saw I could get her, I said the heck with her, I see another one. I'll see if I can get her. And I think I broke a record. I think I had four — how many at once? — as high as five, I know. Right, I was associating with five girls at one time. And none of 'em knew about the other ones really. But then one night at a basketball game they found out.

I think it was the last game of the year, we was in the gym and I was sitting on one side with my main girl. And there was another of my girls sitting on the other side of the gym and she looked across the gym and saw me and she came over to where I was and she sat between me and my main girl. So my main girl said, "Hey, what's this?" She said, "What you call this?" And the other girl, she said, "Well, what's going on, Bobby?" I said, "Nothing." And my other girl said, "What you call this sitting between me and my man?" And this girl sitting in between us, she said, "You and *your* man?" So about that time, I said to myself, "Well, Bobby old boy, I guess it's about time for you to slide on down the way and talk to some of the boys." So I said, "Will you girls please excuse me?"

And I was in the process of going out the back door and one of my other girls was coming from the band room and, man, I didn't know what to do. I felt like going across the basketball court really. And she stopped. Caught me by the arm and pulled me over to the side and she asked me what was I trying to prove. I told her I wasn't trying to prove anything. She said, "You got to be trying to prove something. Sitting over there with another girl." I said, "Well, I'll be back in a minute, I'll be sitting on the bottom bleacher over there."

I'm still trying to get out now, because, you know, the atmosphere is getting thick. Okay, I'm going out the front this time. And another girl, one that I had been taking care of business with, she popped up from the refreshment stand. And I saw her. Heck! I'm gone. And coming out the door, another one that I had been nursing, I saw her sister's car driving by. I thought, "God knows, I hope she isn't in there, this is too much. Heck, I can't stand this." But she was, and they drove by and stopped and backed back and she said, "Bobby, I want to see you." I said, "Okay, I'll be right back. I got a headache, going down to the café." And in less than a week's time I lost five girls.

. . .

How come I'm not sure I want to be in a picture with this house in it too? Because it's not the type of home that I'd want to see in a book, that I would live in, you know. But it's just like I feel . . . I can't help it. That's what my grandmother tells me. Sometime I would get disgusted. I would say, "Heck, I'm gon get me a home as soon as I get out of school. I'm not going to college, trade school, or *anything*, I'm just going to work and get me a home." She would say, "No, go on to school and you'll come out better. You can't help the way you're living now, and you shouldn't feel too bad about it." It's just not the type of thing I want to see in a book, or any place. But my grandmother said I can't help it and I couldn't, but I'm in a position now where I can.

See, I'm planning on building a house right here where this one is, right

on this land, because we own it. See, I think it was my grandmother's aunt who owned this place and she died in about 1960. And her wish was for my grandmother to live here until she could get in contact with her brother, so we moved in. See, this is — how do you pronounce it? — this is heir property. I think there was three owners. And two of the owners is dead, passed on, shall I say, gone to the sweet beyond. And the third is my grandmother's brother. And he's supposed to be in Florida, and we're still in the process of trying to get in contact with him so we can get us a home built. See, my grandmother talked with the county clerk about a month ago and he told her she couldn't have the deeds changed on this property to her name because it was heir property and one of the owners was still living. But we believe something has happened to her brother. Because, you know, naturally if you got relatives you gon want to keep in contact, right? Okay, so no contact, no communications whatsoever, and they're very fond of each other. We've tried the police, we've tried the sheriff, and they can't get in touch with him.

So now that I'm out of school, I'm going in it myself. I'll get my grandmother a lawyer and we'll talk about it and see what we can come up with. I want to dig into this thing. I'm gon try to get it deeded over, because I've always thought that no matter what type of property it was, if the individual made the tax payments for it for seven years, it automatically becomes the payer's property. So I'm gon do that and then I'm gon try to get a home built.

— Was building a home here your idea or your grandmother's?

Mine. And I think I've got enough people behind me to start, and if I start, I know I can get help. For one's my grandmother in Florida. I talked with her about it last summer and she said she'd back me up in whatever I wanted to do, go to school or whatever. And you've got the principal out here, he'll back me up 100 percent.

.   .   .

— What type of toilet facilities does this house have?

Outside. The southern type is outside — which I very rarely use.

— What do you do?

Oh, usually I go to my grandfather's — he lives a few blocks from here — and during the time I'm there if I have to use the bathroom, I use his.

— Why do you not use your outside one?

Just I'm not accustomed to it. And I just don't feel right using an outside toilet.

— Where do you get your water?

From a faucet outside.

— Would you like a spigot inside?

Would I like a faucet inside, a sink? Yes. I would like all the facilities of a complete home. Faucet, bathroom, living room, den, bedroom, closets, because my mother's got all this and when I go down . . . I'll put it this way: If I lived in the Martinique Motel in Columbus, I would know how to carry myself. You know, because I've been accustomed to . . . well, really different ways of living in life. And even here, I carry myself just as I would in what I would call a complete home, because I know how.

I've got a lot of very respectable friends, their mothers and uncles and so forth and school teachers and, you know, they're pretty high in society. And a lot of people don't even know that I live here, because when they see me I'm always neat, and from the way a person carry hisself, you can imagine what type of home he live in, you know. And I just got a lot of friends that just doesn't even know where I live. Well, I will come out and say really the majority of times, I will be ashamed to bring my friends around. There are a lot of girls, just personal girlfriends, say, "Bobby, do you have a phone?" I would say no. They would say, "Well, we're gon come by your house and pick you up and ride around and see some friends," and so forth. I would say, "No, meet me at the hangout." Something like that.

— Has your present girlfriend been over here?

Yeah, she came by. And what was her reaction? I know you was getting ready to ask that question. She didn't seem shocked. That's one thing that I like about this girl and I guess that's what make me love her so much. She look at *me*, you know; she looks at Bobby. And she accepted it and that was good enough for me.

— Where do the nine people that live here sleep?

Well, the house has three rooms — two regular rooms and a kitchen. And three sleep in the front room — me, my grandmother, and the little girl. And then in the other room you've got my father and his wife and the real little kid sleep with them. And the three little boys, they sleep in a bed in the kitchen.

— Do you ever want more privacy?

Yes. I like to read a lot. That's why when I was mentioning a complete home, I mentioned the den. I would like a home where I could go into the den and maybe have a small library, and I like to concentrate. And I like to read literature and usually when I read I like to be able to concentrate on what I'm reading and think about it. And around here, you can't do that.

•　　•　　•

— Describe the difference between the houses of most black people and those of most white people.

Most white people are able enough to live in comfortable homes and blacks are not. Most blacks does not have the facilities of a complete home because they can't afford it. Most blacks aren't given a job to buy what they need for their home.

•   •   •

If you want me to give my opinions on poverty, I got a poem I wrote a few months ago that just about says it all.

I Wonder Why

Through the tears of a terrible plight
I look at the kids as they cry at night.
A baby boy with no clothes to wear.
Papa's no good and everyone knows, cause
His kids are barefoot the whole day through.
A little girl crying, cause she got the flu.
No one cares if they live or die.
And I wonder why, I wonder why.
Why people live in houses so cold.
Cracks in the wall let the wind blow through.
Leak in the roof let the rain in too.
Listen, who heard the little girl cry.
Ice on the ground says winter's here.
I wonder why, as I watch the little girl tears.
I wonder why, I wonder why.
Why people have to live in houses so cold.
Fighting the winter and being so bold.
I wonder why, I wonder why.

•   •   •

— Do you believe anyone powerful cares about poor people?

Yes. I've heard a lot of the senators and so forth argue about welfare and commodities and so forth, and I've heard some that back it 100 percent. They say that the people in America need help. And I've heard some that was against it. They said that it was draining the government of money — which is, I think, *totally downright stupid!* You spend a billions of dollars on rockets. Heck, why not use that money to help the people in America? So why grumble when a man comes up and say, "We'll make up a budget so we can help the poor people."

Bobby Gaines

And then this other man said, "No, don't do that. That will run our budget too low." Whereas when they get ready to make a rocket, something out of metal, doesn't have feeling, they'll go to the limit. Say, "Build it, put whatever it needs, any amount that it needs, put it in there." I don't think that makes much sense.

· · ·

— What is the total income for the nine people that live here?

Well, I think my father makes about seventy-five dollars a week. If he doesn't have any trouble with the rain, I should say. If it rains, no work. No work, no pay. See, he's a pulpwood worker, drives a timberjack. If it rains the entire week, then you'll start getting a few strands of gray hair from worrying, you know, where will the money come from. Like when it rain and he'll maybe get in only two days of work, he'll say, "Heck, I don't have enough, what will I do? After I buy food, there won't be too much left. How will I pay the loan, how will I pay the doctor bill?"

And my grandmother, she gets her pension and security, which comes to over a hundred a month. I don't know the exact amount.

— Is it hard to make ends meet with this amount of income?

Well, as I said, we own this old place, don't have to pay rent or anything and it's not very hard. We keep the type of food a family should have to make a balanced diet and we keep that type of food here. And don't anyone fall behind on their bills too much. And that keeps the money soaked up, so they haven't been able to start doing anything on the house. And I think that's where I come in. I want to be the hero of this thing.

— Do you get commodity foods?

My grandmother does, yes. I was against it.

— Why?

Well, she said that it helps. And I think maybe it does. But I just don't agree with it, because I'm not *totally* helpless, we're not totally helpless. And to me I think people need it who are totally helpless, people that can't get food, the type of food they need.

— Have you done anything to make money recently?

Yeah. At school I cleaned up and got a little for that. Wax the cafeteria, buff the floor, and so forth. And when I was down and out, broke, flat busted, some of my raps would let me hold something till I got some money.

— I guess you have never done any farming . . .

No, I completely dislike farming. It doesn't pay, not for the employee. Huh-

I'm Somebody Important

uh, he doesn't make *nothing,* but the owner, the employer, now he get a little profit if he's had a good year; if not, then he sunk. I don't like farm work, logging, pulpwood, any type of unskilled labor. I prefer profitable business, something that has a good foundation. And I'd like to someday invest my money in some type of stock.

· · ·

— What type of work do you think you might go into?

Well, that's where this going to trade school comes in. To me, you've just about got to have a education. To illustrate that, who gets the highest pay, a man with a degree or a man without a degree? So I wanted an education because I saw the demand for educated people. That's why I like to read the papers and look at news — I saw the demand for educated people. Now, a person with a high school diploma have a chance to live, but he just do get by. But in order to make enough to get by and have some left, you've got to have some type of degree. I felt like I could go to college and succeed. So if I can, then why not go on and do it if you know you gon need it?

So I'm probably — I've just about decided — gon take a two-year course in textile technology at Southern Tech in Marietta, get the money from some funds that the state has reserved to help fellows that they feel . . . well, need it. I'm thinking strongly about it for the fall. I was sort of undecided, but at graduation we had a darn good speaker and that man sort of shook me. He said, "Don't stop now; advance." We got a school motto; our school motto was "Nothing is achieved by retreating; advance through education." Which, if I may compliment myself — which I don't do too much — I wrote. They said they needed a motto since this is the last class be graduating from our school — next year the white school and our school coming together. And I'm pretty good — I would say I was blessed for using my head towards writing and speaking politically, any kind of way, and so they asked me to come up with a motto.

— Before you heard the graduation speaker, what were you thinking about doing?

Just going to work. As you can see from the things that I've said, I've been through enough and I want to get some of the good things from life — quick. So I get out and work and get some things. I want some things that would belong to *me.* But I thought, said, "Dog, if I can get me a degree I could get more of those things." That's what persuaded me.

— How did you decide to take courses in textile technology?

Well, actually, I had planned on going for full four years. I wanted to be a physical education teacher, a coach. I love sports and I love to see young people

get out on the field and participate in sports. And I just like working along with other people, other kids. But this Arrow Company sent a letter to the principal asking him did he have any black students that he felt were qualified to take a course in textile engineering and pass. If so, they would like to aid them, because there was a great demand for black people in their company to hold some pretty big jobs. So he gave it to the counselor and she called me in and told me about it. And she said that the company would pay for the first semester and afterwards they would give you a job. But the thing that sounded good to me the most was the pay. She said it was highly possible that you could make $4.75 starting pay, going to $5.50 an hour. And I think that's pretty good.

Well, I gave it deep thought, about as much thought as a person could have gave something of that nature, because, you know, it was a critical point. And I thought about it for maybe a week. That was the first thing that I'd ever thought real seriously about. And I looked at the teacher's pay now, which is not too good, and I looked at the possibilities of me getting this textile degree and I would be making far more than a teacher would make. And I believe I would like the work.

— What kind of work do you think you would *most like* to do?

I had an ambition to play football. That was one of the things that I wanted to do most, but I had to give that up.

— Why?

Well, if I went to the right school I believe I would have a chance to make it. See, I wanted to play pro football. And I believe I could have made the college team because I'm a pretty strong boy and I've played it before and I know I could play good. But I would have to go to a school that was good football material, that the pros look at, and I can't go to that type of school. So I just counted it out.

— Do you think you have a good chance of making good?

I guess I will make it as good as the next guy, or better, because I've got a lot of determination. I've got a lot of faith in myself, and I believe if you've got faith in yourself, you can carry yourself a long way.

•   •   •

— What do you think you'll be doing and where do you think you'll be living five years from now?

I think I'll be living here . . . I guess. I want to get me a big beautiful home here and . . . just work around here. Maybe not work right here, but somewhere not too far.

Bobby Gaines

— Where would you work?

Maybe Albany . . . But I don't know really. I would *like* to live here. But so far this company, they've said they wanted these black students to work in either Birmingham or Atlanta. But I like a small town, because it's quiet and you can live comfortable. If you've got a good salary. But the big city, it's too much noise, too many people. How do you say it? — there's too much air pollution. I like fresh air . . . But if I have to work there, then I guess that I'll live there. But I'll have a home here also, because I want to see my grandmother in a comfortable place and thereby I'll also have a place to stay myself, so if I feel like coming down here, I can jump in a car or maybe catch a plane or bus and come down.

— Are there any other advantages of living in a small town like Baxter?

No, that's about it. As I said, it's nice and quiet. But in a small town when you get some black haters, it's bad. But otherwise it's okay. You just feel most comfortable because you can live a nice quiet sociable life.

— Are there black haters here?

Yeah, you've got quite a few. Because, you know, in a small town, you're closer together. And when you get black haters close together with blacks, then you've got a mess.

— What are some other disadvantages of living in Baxter?

Getting a job. That's about the worst thing. There's a lumber company here where a lot of guys that get out of school want a job at. But if they want a job there, they'll have to wait until somebody's fired or somebody quit and it's mostly occupied by elderly people. So I would say jobs is about the worst thing about this place.

I guess maybe ten or fifteen kids left here the same night we had graduation, and we had two or three to leave before they ever got diplomas. Why? It's nothing to stay around here for.

.   .   .

— If you could be born as someone else, who would you like to be?

If I could be born as someone else, I wouldn't want to be — I really mean this — if I could be born as Rockefeller, I don't think I'd want to be. If I could be born as President Nixon or Kennedy or King, I wouldn't want to be. I think Bobby Gaines has had an interesting life. I think Bobby Gaines has made a lot of achievements that a lot of people haven't made. And Bobby Gaines wants to build himself, you know.

.   .   .

— Now I want to ask you some questions about race.

Shoot away. That's what I been waiting for. That's one thing I really like to shoot the bull on.

— Are you interested in the race problem?

Am I interested? Very much so. Because I think I'm involved. Because whatever comes from whatever race problem that develops, then that will be a bearing on me. Say, if every white man started running private supermarkets, private drugstores, and all this nature for whites only, then I'd be out of luck. If I get sick I couldn't go to the drugstore. Racial issues, yes, they do affect me because, like I said, I feel part of them. And I feel that if the black man succeeds in an issue or conflict, then I feel as if I have succeeded. If he fails, if he's defeated, then I feel the same way.

— Do you think of these things very often?

You mean do I think about racial issues much? Well, yes, because it makes me feel sort of down to know that here's another human being doesn't want to be around me, doesn't want to associate with me, doesn't want to sit at the same table with me. And this reflects on me; that's just telling me they're against me. I think about that quite often. I say to myself — why? Why he doesn't want to do these things. I'm a human being, I'm made out of the same things he's made out of. The same man that put him here also put me here. So why he can't accept this? And I think about it quite a lot.

— When did you first become aware that white people are like what you just described?

I will say as soon as I entered my teens and got to the point where I could understand something about life. Then I realized that I wasn't being given a chance to do anything, a chance to be anybody, really. Then I found out that I wasn't considered on the same basis as these white people were. I would say as soon as I reached my teens and was able enough to understand, then I realized it.

— What's the first specific thing you can remember that made you start wondering about it?

I think the greatest Negro I can remember, Dr. King, started this realization in me that I wasn't up to the same standards as a white. During the late fifties, I think, I had seen him march in the paper and protest Negroes not having a right to ride on buses with whites. And when I got in my teens, then I put it all together, you know. I said, "Well, King was trying to do this and he was trying to do that." This is what he was working for, the equality of the black man. And then I realized that I was sort of behind and, like I said, when I got to my teens I started putting these things together that I had seen in the past that show preju-

dice and then I learned what the word *prejudice* meant and I was able to understand.

— How do you feel toward white people in general?

In general, I recognize a white man as a human being. And by recognizing
them as a human being, I look upon them as . . . well, somewhat as I would a
Negro. You got some that are nice, you get some that foolish, you got some that
are messy and dirty. In general, I just look at them as human beings. If you treat
me right, I'll treat you right. You treat me like an ass, I'll treat you like an ass.

— What do you think of whites who want to hold blacks down?

I think they need their butts kicked. Because the black has a right to live
and enjoy things. He has just as much right to do that as a white man does, and
why keep them down, they're human. They've got blood just like the whites. The
only thing that is different is the complexion, and then again you've got some
Negroes with complexion almost like whites, so why try to keep them down? So
as far as coming down to say how do I feel about the whites keeping the Negroes
down, I think they should have their butts kicked.

— Do you think most whites look upon you as human as you do them?

Most whites? No, I don't think they look upon me as a human being. Because most whites, they've got this thing where they don't want to associate with
a black man. And from that I'll say they don't look upon me as a human being.

— Why do you think they are like that?

Because they've been taught that way. They've been taught that way in the
past, their parents has told them, "Don't associate with that dirt." And, you
know, whatever you teach a child, he's gon try to live up to those standards. And
that's what has happened; their foreparents has taught them that they're better
than we are, so naturally they feel that way.

— Tell me about some prejudiced whites you know.

Well, there's one that owns this grocery store. He wrote an article about
Negroes for the *Baxter Times* a couple of years ago and the thing bugged me.
He said that a Negro wasn't good for anything but to work and these niggers
are raising sand about this and that and they don't know what they want. And
it was a whole lot of *junk*. That's what I call it, pure junk. When I read that,
I was wishing something would happen to him really. I know it's terrible, but I
was sort of wishing that he would run into a low-flying jet.

— Do you know him personally?

Do I know him personally? Close up, no. But, you know, I've been in his
store and he laughs in their faces; he might as well. You know, you have a lot
of Negroes that have accounts with him. And a lot of elderly Negroes, when they

get their welfare checks or their old folks' pension, they go to him to cash it. And he tell them to their face, I'll do this for you and I'll do that for you, like give 'em a charge account or loan 'em money. But then he comes back and write an article in the paper about Negroes are dumb, don't associate with 'em.

— Does your family have a charge account with him?

My grandmother does. And, naturally, I've tried to talk her out of it, holding an account with him. But she says — which is true — she's got to eat. And between the time she get her checks, she said, it help her out. So I cut it short, I didn't say anything else about it. But me, personally, I don't go there. When she asks me to go, I ask would she send one of the kids, because I'll show how I feel if I go around, you know.

— Have you had any other experiences with bigoted whites?

No. There have been maybe a couple of times when I go to supermarket or drugstore or some place and make a purchase and they would put the change in

Bobby Gaines 229

the hand of the white person in front of me. But me, when I got there, they would take it and lay it on the counter, and I would say, "You stuck up." You know, that's what I would say to myself.

— Do white people around here ever refer to a black man as "boy"?

Yes. And I hate to hear a white man address a Negro or black man as "boy." He's got a name, call him by his name. I've heard a few farmers say it and I have also walked by a few farmers saying, "That nigger I got out there works good." And you know what it does for me? It makes me feel like taking him and putting him in a barrel of boiling oil.

— When you have to refer to the race of a person, which term do you prefer — black, Negro, or colored?

Colored burns me up, because I saw that word too many times when I was growing up. "Colored Only." "No Colored Allowed." And that thing sort of dug in, you know, and I just don't like the word. I would rather be recognized as a Negro by white people, but my friends, I like to be recognized by them as black.

— Why?

I just don't like to hear white persons use the term, call me black, because in the past I heard them describe Negroes — "*Black* this, *black* that," you know, like it's dirt or something. You know, "That black *nig-ger* this, that black *nig-ger* that." And, man, it tore me up.

But amongst other black people, I like to hear the word *black,* because they say it as if they are proud of it. It's just a way that black people say it to each other, you know. It develops a sense of pride. But to hear a white man say it is something else. He throw emphasis on it.

— Has a white man ever called you a nigger?

No. If so, I would have been busting rock. I don't like that term. We would have had a good fight, and when I get mad I don't stop until I get satisfaction. And I know if a white person and myself would have got in a fight around here and I would have gotten satisfaction, the other white people wouldn't have liked it. And *believe me,* in these small southern towns when a Negro does something and the white man doesn't like it, he'll do something about it. And he usually won't be alone. And the heck thing about it is, *he* won't be alone, but the Negro will be alone. See, you've got too many black people in the South afraid to stand up for one another. Whereas white people have always stuck beside one another; that's one thing I can credit the white for. As far as the Negro, no, they really haven't stuck together, but it's pulling together, things are coming closer together . . .

. . . Oh! I forgot. I have been called a nigger. I was pretty small, about nine or ten, and it slipped by my memory. But I *never will* forget it because it was a relief and it was a pleasure for me. A crowd of fellows used to hang around the theater — there'd be some white kids and some black. And once, this white fellow came around and said to me and some other fellows out there, "What are you niggers doing out here?" I guess he was trying to show off.

So I've always been where if you insult me, I'll speak out. I've *got* to strike back; if I don't I blow up. So I looked around and said to the fellows with me, said, "Do you guys see any niggers standing around?" And you know how kids are, they are not afraid of anything really, so they said, "No, I don't see any niggers around here." So I looked at this white fellow, I said, "Who are you calling nigger?" And he said, "You, if you want to take it." I said, "Hell no, I don't want to take it. And you can't make me take it. You want to?" I said, "Hello, Cracker." So he slapped me.

When he slapped me, I just politely asked him, "Do you want to fight?" I said, "I dare you to step behind the theater." So he said, "C'mon, I'm gon kick your butt." We went back there and we started scrapping. And when I got through beating his butt, I took him and put him in the doggone garbage can and told him that where he need to be, in there with the trash, you know, because he didn't respect me. I've always had a great deal of pride. And if he didn't respect me, then the hell with him, I didn't respect him.

— You said kids are not afraid of anything; are you afraid of any whites around here now?

Am I afraid of any? I'll say this from my heart — no, nowhere!

— Are most young black people from this area like you, or are they more afraid of whites?

The young people my age, they are very high-spirited. If you get them riled up, they don't care, they'll stand up for their rights. I'll vouch for the young people my age, especially the ones that live in town. They'll stand up, they're high-spirited. But there seems to be a drawback with the ones that live in the country. They seem afraid.

— Could you give me an example of a young person living in the country who wouldn't stand up?

If I may, first of all let me say why I believe they are like that. In the country you got a lot of Negroes that's working on the farm, and they're staying on a white man's property. And they know if they don't go along with what this white man say, they will have to move. They will be out of a home and out of a job. So if the white man say do this, then the young person's parents will say go along

with him. They might not want to, but their parents will tell them to, because they know if he don't they will be thrown out of their home. So that's the reason why I think most of the kids in the country are sort of timid toward coming out and speaking their opinions.

And have I seen any example? you asked me. Well, I will say I haven't came upon a direct issue where they was afraid, but I've noticed it from observation. I'm good at observation; I observe a lot of things people think that normally people don't observe. Say I'll see a boy come to town with his bossman; he's dirty, grease all over him, dust all over him. The man say, "John, do this." "Yassir, yassir." And that burns me up, you know. And he jump to it like if he don't do it in a hurry, the man will hit him or something. And if you observe enough, you can only come to that conclusion, that they're afraid.

— Will many adult black people in this area stand up to white people?

Yes, you got quite a few that will. Like one time the furniture man came by and my father hadn't got off work and the man started cursing at my father's wife, saying that he was gon get the damn furniture if he didn't hurry up and get some money, and the payments wasn't even behind. And when the man came back, my father told him, said, "Look, man, I don't like the way you did to my wife. You wouldn't want me cursing you wife. I want you to respect my wife just as I would respect yours." And they had it out and so my father told him to get off his property.

And then one time . . . This was sort of funny. My father had gotten a month behind on his payment to the loan company. So the man came down and started talking about he would take his furniture and send the cops down and all that. So Pop just told him, say, "I'll bring your money up there next week, man." So the man didn't want to settle for it and he started talking strong, and I had one of those pump air rifles sitting by the door. So Pop said, "I tell you what you do, you get out of my house." So the man kept on talking and Pop reached for the BB gun and I guess the guy thought it was a real gun, you know, one that would do some damage, and he took off.

And then you've got quite a few adults in town that will come up to the white and say, "We don't like that, we don't want it, you got to do something better." And I think King contributed to that.

We've got the president of the PTA, he's a civil rights worker. That man will stand up and tell *any* white man that my people doesn't want this, my people doesn't want that, they don't want to hear it. They're not going to have any more sports next year because of this integration thing when the two schools come together. And the president of the PTA got up in this meeting, he said, "Mr. Board Chairman, we will *not* let our kids go to school if it doesn't have sports." And I admire that. They asked the board chairman, "Why? Why didn't he want sports?" And he couldn't even give a concrete reason as to why.

— What do you think is his reason?

What do I think the reason is? I think the man don't want that black girl and that black boy and that white girl and that white boy being in the same place together. I don't think he want to see them in the showers together, or on the floor together, on the court together, or ride in the same bus to play different schools together. I don't think he want to see that. That's why I believe he did it. That's why a lot of people believe he did it. But if he would only ask, he would find out that the Negro, the black people, feel the same way. If you don't want my kid there, I don't want him there either. Because just like the white consider their kids angels, so does the black people. They consider their kids angels.

See, the whites say they don't want their kids going to school with a black kid. Well, the blacks feel the same way; they don't want their kids going to school with whites. In this town, I can say that most of the black people feel the same way. They say heck, if that white man don't want his daughter going to school with my son, then I don't want my son going to school with his daughter or his son. They might integrate, sure, but they'll do it because they're forced to.

— Your school has not been integrated . . .

No, which I'm sort of glad of. Next year it will be.

— Why are you glad?

Because the way things are we probably would have had demonstrations and probably would have had violence and they probably would have had to close the school down and then a lot of kids would have been out of an education. Whereas they might have graduated this year they'll have to go somewhere else or stay here and go to school again next school term. And I just wouldn't have wanted to see what would happen.

— Who would have done the demonstrating?

You probably would have had the parents of some white kids, and then that would have brought the Negro out also. And then when you get, you know, two different races together and they are angry with one another, a conflict is going to start.

— Just imagine that you had known for sure there would have been no conflict; would you have wanted your school to be integrated or not?

If I knew that anything wouldn't of happened, I would say yes, it would be okay for whites to come to our school, because for people to get to know other people, you've got to associate with them some. And I think that going to school together will definitely help a person to know another person, know something about them. It will let them know that as many Negroes as they believe is ignorant isn't ignorant.

— You've been saying white parents don't want their children to go to school with blacks — how do you think the children feel?

Well, I'll tell you about the white kids and I'd say the same is true for the black kids. I might be making a big mistake, a hell of a mistake, but I would say the white kids don't feel like their parents. I would say they want to come, because I believe they just like the kids at my school; see, the kids at my school want to learn about whites. And I think a lot of white kids, especially in the last ten years, they want to learn something more about Negroes because they're curious. The young people now, they are *far* more curious than people were a long time ago.

Bobby Gaines   235

— Do you think young white people are different from their parents?

Very much so. As far as treating Negroes — blacks — more as if they are human beings, they are. They seem to want to associate with blacks more than their parents did. You know, actually, their mother's mother was back there when the Negro was way down and they would tell them pretty horrible stories of what the Negro is, what they think he stands for, and that's embedded in their parents' mind and, you see, that became a part of them. And whereas their kids were born in a far advance time than they were. And their kids have a chance to see Negroes as senators and mayors and Negro politicians and a Negro with high standings, and they wonder. They say, "Now if Mama say the Negro was this and that, stupid and so forth, why is he there? I'm curious."

— Do you think there is much job discrimination here?

Well, yes. Because you can go in most of the stores, do you see any black clerks? Do you see any black people working in drugstores, druggists? Do you see any black people holding a job as foreman? Well, all the higher-paying jobs is being occupied by whites.

— How do you feel about whites in general having money while blacks don't have very much?

Well, I will say it's just a thing as to where the white man used his head, the Negro was using their back. I feel as if the Negro got the white man what he has now. Look at the cotton plantations they had. Who worked 'em? Who put money in this white man's pocket? The Negro. And like I said, during the time that the Negro was using his back, his muscle rather, the white man was just using his head. I look at it this way — I can't feel too bad about it because the majority of the Negroes just started to step forward and get some of the things that they should have had then. But during that time the white man only looked on the Negro — as some of them do now — as an animal, you know, as a domestic animal, and they used them for work purposes. Whereas he couldn't get out and start a small profitable business, because the man kept him working. I would say that Negroes started off from scratch, whereas the white man started off with something in his pocket. That's why I admire Negroes now.

— What changes would you like to see in whites?

What changes? I would like to see them accept the black man as a human being. I would like to see them blend in and try to give the black man a chance. I would like to see them meet a black man and say, "Hello, George," "Hello John," "Hello Sam," "Hello Bob." Just greet me as a person.

•　　　•　　　•

— If you were light enough to pass for white, would you?

If I was light enough to pass for a white, would I? No, I don't believe I would. Because the Negro has something to be very proud of. And I am a Negro. God put me here with my skin black, red, brown, or whatever you want to call it. But I'll say *black,* because I love the word. And I'm here as a black, let me stay here as a black, let me die as a black.

·　　·　　·

— Do you believe any black people ever try to keep fellow blacks down?

Yes. You've got a lot of Negroes that doesn't believe in sticking together. That's commonly said among Negroes when they discuss the issue of keeping one another down and who's keeping who down; they say, "Well, if the Negroes stuck together like the whites, then we might have gotten something." But they seem not to understand that a man has got to try to get what he can, and in the process of him getting what he can, the other man might get the impression he was trying to keep him down. But most blacks say that other blacks keep each other down because they're not sticking together. Which I don't think they should say that either.

·　　·　　·

— Do you think the racial situation has changed during the past five years?

Yes. I think it has changed because it has been so well publicized *nationally.* You know, you got a lot of whites watching the news and so forth, and they see the Negro in the North or in the deeper South marching or demonstrating against something, which the white know is right. So they never had it here, but by them seeing it and thinking it over, well, they *know* the man is right. They see the man is right, so maybe they say here we'll try and go as far as we can with accepting him.

— What do you think white people around here think of advances by black people?

Well, I think they are surprised, for one thing. I don't believe people around here thought that a Negro could advance as far as they have. And I don't think they too much like it, because Negroes are getting too close to the standards of whites. And I don't think that they like that because they believe that a Negro is suppose to always stay at the ass end of something.

But you can take a jar and fill it with water and put it in the refrigerator. Well, that temperature will get so low until that jar bursts. Okay, that's pressure. So the Negro has taken so much pressure until they've got to burst out, they've got to come out and say, "Look, man, I'm woke now." And I don't think they have until recently when the Negroes started standing up, stepping out of the gutters, and speaking up.

— Would you like a civil rights organization in Baxter?

Yes, I would. As a matter of fact, I thought about that, I think, last year in my junior year. I thought about maybe if they had some type of Negro organization here, it would help some of the Negroes. Because, you know, these organizations, they focus their actions on one thing — getting better things for Negroes. And if one was here, you know, they could work direct with the people. And I think it would be pretty good.

— Would you join a demonstration if one were organized here?

If a demonstration was organized for a concrete purpose and I felt like the people had a reason to be there, yes, I would join. Say, for instance, if they send more white teachers over here and less Negro teachers over there — if they marched against that, I'd be for it.

Yes, I think demonstrations do some good. They draw people's attention. Somebody might get hurt, somebody might end up in jail, but it'll get attention. Make a man say, "Well, let's sit down and talk then." So, yes, I think they serve a good purpose.

— What do you think about violence as a tactic to correct injustices?

I don't agree with violence. I think if things can be agreed upon by nonviolence, then I believe they should. It's this way: The war we're in now, there's Communist aggression rising. And so that's wrong, and they had to try to correct it with violence. Well, if you don't have any other alternative but to use violence, then I guess you'll have to do it. But just to come down and say I believe things could be or should be corrected through violence, no. If you can do it in a peaceful way, then do it. But you got to do it some way.

●　　●　　●

— What black leader do you admire most?

That'd be Abernathy, Ralph Abernathy. Along with a lot of black people, we consider Abernathy *the* man to have taken the seat after King. Which is a very high position as you get nationally known in it. And the Negroes feel that he's their leader. If something happen, something that's against the Negro, Abernathy's there. Say if anything happen here, you would send for and ask Abernathy to come down, you would describe the problem to him, go into details, and he would come down and get the people and have a meeting and so forth. And he's just a leader.

Bobby Gaines

— How did you feel when Martin Luther King was killed?

I felt as if a part of me had been taken away from me, like someone had taken a knife and just sliced part of me off. King was sort of a big image to the black people. Most blacks thought as if King was part of them. Just as most blacks, I felt, "This is it." If the white man want to take my leader away from me, then the heck with him, the hell with him, if you wanna fight we'll fight. At the moment I heard it I felt this way, but afterward I said, "No, that doesn't make any sense, Bobby, the man worked for peace all his life and so just believe in what the man worked for."

— Have you ever thought about being a civil rights leader?

Well, yes, it's crossed my mind a couple of times. I thought about it last year; I guess last year was my thinking year. I would like to be one, but I don't think I'll ever make it that far. Well, I probably could, but I just couldn't visualize myself that far up. I'd like to be recognized as a hero or leader or helper or whatever you want to call it; I'd like to be recognized among Negroes as that. Which I think a lot of young black people would want to be. But to make it there, I don't know.

·   ·   ·

— What would you most like to change about yourself?

Started to say my looks, but I'm *grateful* for them. If I could change anything about me, what would I want to change? I wouldn't want to change my past definitely, because it shows a young man that was down and came back strong, which is very remarkable for any person. Change about myself as an individual? Really nothing. I'm happy with the way I am.

·   ·   ·

— What are the two things that are worrying you the most?

The two things that are worrying me the most right now? Sometimes I wonder will I be able to make it, will I be able to reach my goal. That's something that comes through my mind quite regularly.

And I guess the destiny of my father's kids, that's one thing that worries me. Because if he's not able to give them what they need now, as time advances, things will get higher, and there will be a higher demand for education and he won't be able to meet this demand.

— What do his children think of you?

Well, they look up to me pretty good. Pretty good, yeah. What I want to do, I want to try to set an example for them. I'd like to see all of them go through school, you know. Especially that young kid, the one that's third from the oldest. He's real smart to be young as he is, he got a lot of pep and, well, his intelligence is showing up. I'd like to see him say, "Well, my big brother, he finished high school. He's gone to college over there and he's doing pretty good." And I think by me carrying myself the way I have, that's helped him to look up to me. And, well, I just like to get him thinking now, you know, and let it grow in him young.

• • •

— When were you the most afraid?

The scardest I've ever been? About three or four months ago I had my girl in a car and Kenneth, a friend of mine, was driving. And we was heading for Sheldon, and we didn't know it but a black in Sheldon had jumped on a white police over there and beat him up in this café, and they had called for other law enforcement officers: state troopers there, sheriff and deputy and city police. And, you know, they had guns, shotguns, and rifles and so forth.

And we was coming through the vicinity where they was, and this guy had a gun on the street. And he was a short guy, and he was stout, and he looked like a black hater. He had a mouthful of tobacco and when we approached him, Kenneth said, "My God, what is this, homeboy?" I said, "I don't know, man." And this guy, he stepped out on the street with his gun and he was in the process of waving us by, but he did wrong and threw the barrel of the gun toward us and waved it in our direction. And my girl was there and she said, "Oh, God, Bobby." I said, "Don't grab me, I can't help you." I slid down in the seat and Kenneth slid down trying to drive, you know, looking up over the dash. And I looked back and the man was showing all his front teeth. He was laughing. It was funny, I knew it was funny to him, but I, you know . . .